THE ARCHAEOLOGY OF ANCIENT EGYPT

Egyptologists, art historians, philologists, and anthropological archaeologists have long worked side by side in Egypt, but they often fail to understand one another's approaches. This book aims to introduce students to the archaeological side of the study of ancient Egypt and to bridge the gap between disciplines by explaining how archaeologists tackle a variety of problems. Douglas J. Brewer introduces the theoretical reasoning for each approach, as well as the methods and techniques applied to support it. This book is essential reading for any student considering further study of ancient Egypt.

Douglas J. Brewer is professor of anthropology at the University of Illinois. He is the author (with Emily Teeter) of *Egypt and the Egyptians*, as well as of numerous other books and articles on Egypt, covering topics from domestication to cultural change and the environment. He has more than thirty years of fieldwork experience in Egypt; currently he is researching the cultures and environment of Egypt's deserts.

THE ARCHAEOLOGY OF ANCIENT EGYPT

Beyond Pharaohs

DOUGLAS J. BREWER
University of Illinois, Urbana-Champaign

CAMBRIDGE
UNIVERSITY PRESS

CAMBRIDGE UNIVERSITY PRESS
Cambridge, New York, Melbourne, Madrid, Cape Town,
Singapore, São Paulo, Delhi, Mexico City

Cambridge University Press
32 Avenue of the Americas, New York, NY 10013-2473, USA

www.cambridge.org
Information on this title: www.cambridge.org/9780521707343

© Cambridge University Press 2012

This publication is in copyright. Subject to statutory exception
and to the provisions of relevant collective licensing agreements,
no reproduction of any part may take place without the written
permission of Cambridge University Press.

First published 2012

Printed in the United States of America

A catalog record for this publication is available from the British Library.

Library of Congress Cataloging in Publication Data

Brewer, Douglas J.
The archaeology of ancient Egypt : beyond pharaohs / Douglas J. Brewer.
    p.   cm.
Includes bibliographical references and index.
ISBN 978-0-521-88091-6 (hardback) – ISBN 978-0-521-70734-3 (pbk.)
1. Egypt – Antiquities.   2. Archaeology – Egypt – Methodology.   3. Egyptology.   I. Title.
DT60.B745   2012
932–dc23   2012012069

ISBN 978-0-521-88091-6 Hardback
ISBN 978-0-521-70734-3 Paperback

Cambridge University Press has no responsibility for the persistence or accuracy of URLs for
external or third-party Internet Web sites referred to in this publication and does not
guarantee that any content on such Web sites is, or will remain, accurate or appropriate.

TO MY WIFE ANN, AND THE BREWER AND PÉREZ FAMILIES,
THANK YOU

CONTENTS

LIST OF ILLUSTRATIONS

LIST OF TABLES

PREFACE

My original vision for this book was that it would be a review of archaeology's contribution to the study of ancient Egypt. The content was to be a simple enumeration of those sites and artifacts that in some profound way influenced our understanding of Egyptian culture. In my discussions with Egyptologists over the various sites to include, it became clear to me that there was a deep frustration with archaeologists, in particular those of us with an anthropological background. As one close friend and colleague said to me, "It is almost as if you archaeologists speak a different language." Obviously, we as archaeologists have done a poor job in explaining our position and goals to our Egyptology colleagues, even when they have worked literally side by side with us in a mosquito-infested excavation pit.

I for one have asked many questions of my Egyptology friends, and they have patiently answered them, and by extending that courtesy have allowed me to have a deeper appreciation and understanding of ancient Egypt. It struck me that perhaps I have not returned the favor. How could my Egyptology-oriented friends be expected to teach archaeology, its methods, and goals to their students, without some support from me (us)? I certainly could not teach subjects in Egyptology without strong support and guidance from them.

I thus changed the focus of the book – away from sites and lists of artifacts to the discipline of archaeology and the method, theory, and techniques commonly applied to retrieve and interpret those artifacts – the idea being that a good Egyptologist, professional or student, will already know the sites and what was found there (or could easily look it up), but might need help in understanding the reasoning behind a particular archaeological question or approach to the data. This difference revolves around the distinctive paradigms followed by the respective fields; that is, whereas the Egyptologist is looking for historical facts, the archaeologist is trying to view a process through time, which requires a different approach – one often not realized by those following a history-bound paradigm (and vice versa). To use an analogy, if a child has misbehaved, one approach would be to look at what that misstep was and how it might be corrected. A different approach might be to look at the long-term path that led to the misbehavior to try and understand why it came to be in the first place. Although the child is the subject of both inquiries, very different approaches and types of data are required to answer the respective questions. Both approaches are certainly valid, and both may solve the immediate problem, but the paths taken are different. So in this text, my goal is to try and explain to students how the archaeological approach (particularly anthropological archaeology) differs from the more historical, Egyptological approach. Thus, the chapters introduce some of the theoretical reasoning for a given approach, as well as the methods and techniques applied to support that approach. Although a number of topics might seem rudimentary to some of my Egyptology colleagues, to others they may not. I am reminded of a statement made by a reviewer of an earlier work of mine, who questioned the need for a chapter on the Nile Valley's environment when discussing Egyptian culture, something this reviewer clearly felt was superfluous. To me, an archaeologist, this was an incredible statement. How could I discuss a culture and its evolution without knowledge of the environment within which it had evolved?

The greatest difficulty in completing this work was to find a series of sites that through a natural progression in time and subject matter would adequately tell the archaeological story. In some instances, this was easy, and in others, it was something of a stretch, but my hope is that the message, the manner in which we as archaeologists approach a problem, has transcended my choice of sites as well as their place in time.

For seasoned Egyptologists who are reading this text for some enlightenment, I do hope you find something here of interest, but the book was not written specifically for you. I envision the audience to be undergraduate students who have already taken an introductory Egyptology course and now need to think about what direction they might want to pursue next: philology, art history, or archaeology, which, of course, are not necessarily mutually exclusive. My hope is that this text might serve as that next step: introducing the student to the archaeological side of the study of ancient Egypt. Ultimately, it would be nice to see this work as part of a trilogy, with an introductory art history and philology text bundled together to assist the interested neophyte at the beginning of his or her scholarly journey.

As is traditional of such books, I have refrained as much as possible from incorporating citations within the text in the hope of making it an easier read for the intended audience. The references on which I have so heavily depended are listed at the end of the text. Although a seemingly simple book,

I am surprised at how long it took me to write it. Throughout the course of this endeavor, there have been many to whom I owe thanks. Beatrice Rehl deserves special thanks for her numerous pep talks and for keeping me focused on the project, especially after I tossed the third completed draft in the trash, vowing never to return to it. Thanks go, too, to Robert Wenke for the innumerable discussions we have had on archaeology throughout the many years of our partnership, which more often than not occurred while we were sitting in a dusty, hot, and miserably uncomfortable vehicle riding to or from our excavation site. Emily Teeter, Donald Redford, Ron Leprohon, Edwin Brock, and a host of other Egyptologists deserve thanks for their frank discussion of archaeology and archaeologists. Finally, a thank you to the National Geographic Society, the Bioanthropology Foundation, and the University of Illinois Research Board, for funding many seasons of fieldwork, with a special thanks to the university for honoring me with a Beckman Award, which allowed me the opportunity to study the Bedouin and to record the ancient rock art in the Eastern Desert.

1

INTRODUCTION: HISTORY AND DEVELOPMENT
OF ARCHAEOLOGY

ARCHAEOLOGY AND EGYPTOLOGY

Archaeology, as defined by the *Oxford English Dictionary*, is the "study of human history and prehistory through the excavation of sites and analysis of physical remains." These physical remains include not only every item ever made by humans – from a piece of burnt charcoal to awe-inspiring stone monuments – but also the remains of humans themselves. As such, archaeology is one of the widest-ranging scientific disciplines and incorporates method and theory from art, history, linguistics, geology, biology, chemistry, mathematics, and the social sciences.

What is Egyptology and how does it differ from archaeology? Egyptology is a historical discipline devoted to the study of ancient Egypt. It is modeled after classical studies of Greece and Rome, which rely on written records to supply chronology, historical data, and information about beliefs of the past. Egyptologists work with specific texts to understand nuances of the ancient culture, often within a well-defined time period. As with all historical disciplines, Egyptology is a particularizing discipline. That is, it is primarily interested in defining what happened at a specific place and time.

Egyptology has an obvious relationship with anthropological archaeology, because both deal with the human past, its narration, and its explanation. Some Egyptologists interested in the development of art and architecture employ archaeological techniques to recover objects, but they analyze them within their own historical (not anthropological) theoretical framework. Texts, too, can provide very specific information on a given time, place, or career of an individual. Archaeology, on the other hand, generally only provides insights into broad processes of change in material culture over long periods of time. Where Egyptology and archaeology really converge is in studies of sites and areas where textual sources, monumental architecture, and objects of art-historical significance are absent, rare, or poorly understood. It is under these circumstances that archaeological methods and techniques take the forefront of Egyptological investigations.

DEVELOPMENT OF A DISCIPLINE

In the West, the scientific discipline of archaeology (and Egyptology as well) has its roots in the Italian Renaissance, when fourteenth-century scholars began to question the origins of the ancient monuments located throughout the Mediterranean region. It was clear that these monuments were built by a civilization prior to Renaissance Europe that in many ways rivaled or even surpassed it. Europeans began traveling to other lands, particularly Italy, Greece, and the Near East, to retrieve ancient objects for their governments' museums or simply to profit from the sale of the pieces. Thus began a collecting spree that continues, at least to some degree, today.

Others with an interest in the past, and who were often driven by a nationalistic ideology, turned their attention to the mounds and monuments within the borders of their own countries. Although neither as overtly spectacular nor as easily recovered as the material remains of the ancient Mediterranean cultures, when subjected to careful study, the artifacts and sites of northern Europe did yield tantalizing clues about their ancient makers. It was this line of discovery, characterized by painstaking recovery and meticulous documentation that laid the foundation for the scientific discipline known today as archaeology.

From Denmark, we see the first systematic classification of artifacts. Building on traditional scholarly divisions of antiquity, C. J. Thomsen of the National Museum of Denmark was the first archaeologist to clearly define the classic Three Age System – Stone, Bronze, and Iron – that would form the basis for all Old World archaeology. Developed and promulgated by Thomsen between 1818 and 1825, the Three Age System was already accepted and used by leading Scandinavian archaeologists by the time it was officially published in 1836. Later, Thomsen's protégé, J. A. A. Worsaae, verified and refined the three-part classification system through careful stratigraphic excavation and analysis.

Yet there were still crucial developments that needed to take place in the fields of geology, biology, and the social sciences before modern archaeology could be born. The first of these was the publication of Charles Lyell's *Principles of Geology* (1830–33), which demonstrated the earth's great antiquity and broke the so-called biblical time barrier for the world's creation (4004 BC). Building on previous work by Cuvier and Hutton and using evidence he gathered in the region around Mt. Etna, Lyell proposed that there are natural explanations for all geologic phenomena, that the ordinary natural processes of today do not differ in kind or magnitude from those of the past (the doctrine of *uniformitarianism*), and that the earth must therefore be very ancient because these processes work so slowly. Although these concepts may seem obvious to us today, they were revolutionary in Lyell's time. In addition to laying out the methods and principles that modern geologists use every day, Lyell's *Principles of Geology* provided a younger group of scholars the opportunity to speculate on time and change.

One young scientist profoundly influenced by Lyell's work was Charles Darwin. Darwin's seminal treatise *The Origin of Species*, published in 1859, expounded on the diversity of life and proposed the mechanism of natural selection for evolutionary change through time. Simply put, he believed that those groups of living organisms best adjusted to the conditions in which they live have the greatest chance for surviving and passing on their traits to the next generation. This concept of natural selection would have great import not only to biologists, but also to scholars interested in explaining cultural change through time.

These two principles – the great antiquity of the earth and natural selection – were soon applied to human and extinct animal remains found in the Somme Valley of France, and for the first time scholars began to accept human coexistence with extinct animals, a fact that many people had refused to believe even when confronted with the clear evidence of stone tools lying juxtaposed with ancient bones. In 1869, soon after the acceptance of this coexistence, the first evidence of prehistoric humans in Egypt was reported: stone tools, tens of thousands of years old, found in the Nile Valley.

During the second half of the nineteenth century, advances in archaeological methods and techniques taking place in the Mediterranean region were turning the field from mere treasure hunting into a more rigorous, scientific discipline. From 1860 to 1875, Giuseppe Fiorelli directed excavations at the site of Pompeii in Italy. He was a progressive and innovative archaeologist who was one of the first to apply the principles of stratigraphy and large-area excavation. Under his guidance, exploration became more methodical, record keeping was improved, and frescoes were left in place rather than removed. He was also responsible for the now-famous plaster casts of Pompeii's victims. Perhaps most importantly, Fiorelli began a training school for archaeological methods, providing a resource for many future archaeologists. In Britain, A. H. L. Fox Pitt Rivers excavated Roman and Saxon sites with military rigor and precision during the last two decades of the nineteenth century. Influenced by Darwin's work, Pitt Rivers developed his own parallel theory of cultural evolution and applied it to his extensive collection of archaeological and ethnographic material, but his most important methodological innovation was his insistence that plain, everyday objects were the key to understanding the past.

A generation younger than Fiorelli and Pitt Rivers, the man who arguably did the most to usher archaeology into the modern era was Sir William Flinders Petrie, and his almost six decades of work in the Middle East remains unsurpassed. From 1880 to 1938, Petrie surveyed and excavated numerous sites in Egypt and Palestine including Giza, Tanis, Naukratis, and Daphnae in the Nile Delta, the Fayum, Thebes, Abydos, Amarna, Naqada, the Sinai peninsula, and Tell Hasi in Palestine. In 1904, Petrie published *Method and Aims in Archaeology*, the definitive work of his time. But he is perhaps best known for building a chronology based on stylistic changes in artifacts he excavated from cemeteries in Upper Egypt. This method of relative dating, known as sequence dating, would prove invaluable to archaeologists working to build chronologies without recourse to historical records. In particular, New World archaeologists seized upon this technique because the indigenous cultures of the Americas either did not have written language or, as in the case of the Maya, their written language was as yet undecipherable.

Although the nineteenth century can be characterized by the initial development of archaeological methods and techniques, the twentieth century can be characterized by the development of archaeological theory. In the Old World, archaeology was basically an outgrowth of history, and the archaeologists were generally historians looking at material culture. In the New World, on the other hand, archaeologists were more closely affiliated with ethnographers and cultural anthropologists because they were excavating sites that belonged to the direct ancestors of the living peoples whom the anthropologists were studying. Thus, it was perfectly natural for the New World archaeologists to work closely with the anthropologists and borrow their theoretical perspective. At first this distinction had very little practical impact, as both the historical archaeologists and the anthropological archaeologists were primarily interested in constructing cultural chronologies of their respective regions, but by the middle of the twentieth century, the two types of archaeology began to diverge. Anthropologists, and by extension anthropological archaeologists, began to focus on questions of process – the "how" and "why" of culture change, in addition to the historical questions of "what," "when," and "where."

ARCHAEOLOGICAL THEORIES OR PARADIGMS

There are few words more misunderstood or used to mean different things than the word "theory." To most nonscientists, "theory" and "hypothesis" are often – incorrectly – used interchangeably, but even among scientists (particularly social scientists) there is considerable variation in how the term is used. Although many practitioners of archaeology use "theory" to refer to the approach to their discipline's subject matter, the concept of paradigm may actually be more appropriate. Developed by historian of science Thomas Kuhn and defined in his book *The Structure of Scientific Revolutions* (1962), a paradigm determines (1) what is to be observed and studied, (2) what kind of questions are to be asked and how they are structured, (3) how an experiment is to be conducted, and (4) how the results of scientific investigations should be interpreted.

It must be noted that Kuhn himself felt that the term "paradigm" was not appropriate for the social sciences, and in fact developed the concept while surrounded by social scientists and observing that they were never in agreement on theories or concepts. (Having experienced more than my fair share of just such gatherings, I sympathize with Kuhn. Most of us finding ourselves in similar situations, simply retire to our rooms after a few stiff drinks; one cannot but admire Kuhn's genius and fortitude under such adverse conditions.) Kuhn's intentions notwithstanding, today the term "paradigm" is used widely in both the social and natural sciences to denote an explanatory model or conceptual framework, and it is this meaning that I intend in the following discussion.

There are three main paradigms at work in archaeology today: culture history, processualism, and post-processualism. Each developed as a reaction to perceived deficiencies in the previous paradigm, but none has completely supplanted the others. Indeed, all three have made and still make contributions to our understanding of the past.

CULTURE HISTORY

Culture history emerged in the nineteenth century and, as the name suggests, it is closely allied with the field of history. Its primary goal is describing the "what," "when," and "where" of past peoples, based on the material record.

By describing and classifying assemblages of artifacts through design style, geographic distribution, and time, culture historians group sites into distinct "cultures." (A culture in archaeological terms is the material manifestation of the people that created the artifacts.) Using inductive reasoning, culture historians identify common themes between cultures, which in turn lead to the construction of overarching narratives to explain the past.

Creating culture histories through archaeology is fairly straightforward and accurate, particularly when one deals with periods where written records are preserved. Histories are made by first amassing large collections of artifacts (pottery, mud-brick buildings, stone-lined tombs, stone and metal tools, etc.) and then making enlightened inferences about the relationships between the people who created the artifacts. Modern forms of dating have helped arrange these collections in time, but most inferences are still made by comparing artifacts.

For example, from my own experience investigating the early Predynastic period of the Egyptian Delta, our crew went from site to site collecting samples of pottery, charcoal, and anything else we could recover from the surface of some thirty sites. Using an auger, we collected buried materials, some as deep as 17 meters below the surface. At the end of each day we examined the pottery and other artifacts for similarities and differences. Based on the assumption that sites with the most similar types of pottery and other datable artifacts were most closely related in time, we constructed a rough map of settlements for Egypt's east central Delta, noting where and when sites first appeared and how they expanded in size and shifted localities through time. We were able to re-create our early settlement history of this area because the pottery types are relatively well known and can be associated with a particular period of time. Of course, our culture history of this region is only as precise as the dates traditionally attributed to the pottery we recovered and our ability to identify the pottery properly.

PROCESSUALISM

Most archaeologists recognize that "description" is what creating histories is all about. Culture historians do an excellent job of classifying items and constructing chronologies, but they do not attempt, at least in a theoretical sense, to explain how or why those artifacts came to be. Addressing such questions is the intent of processual archaeology.

Presaged by Walter Taylor's critique of culture history, and articulated by Gordon Willey and Philip Phillips in their 1958 classic *Method and Theory in*

Archaeology, the idea that archaeology should be the study of cultural process, not just culture history, began to take hold in American circles. Proponents of this "New Archaeology" claimed that with the rigorous use of the scientific method, specifically the hypothetico-deductive model, it was possible to get past the limits of the archaeological record and actually reconstruct the lifeways of the people who made and used the artifacts. The assumption on which processual theory is based is that of cultural evolution – the belief that culture is an extrasomatic means of environmental adaptation for humans. As such, processualists believe that culture change is not only understandable, but also objectively predictable once the interaction of the variables is understood. With the work of Louis Binford in the 1960s and Kent Flannery in the 1970s, processual archaeology became the dominant theoretical model for archaeology in America.

As an example of processual archaeology, when conducting research on the ancient shores of Lake Qarun in the Fayum, I recovered an enormous number of fish bones. Most of these bones came from fish crania. The common explanation for this pattern was, given the large size of these fish, that the ancient Fayum fishermen removed the head (which had little meat) and left it at the lake, transporting the rest of the fish to a camp or home site for further processing and eating. Other equally viable explanations exist, however. First, the skull bones of fish are far more numerous than postcranial skeletal bones. Second, cranial bones are easier to identify taxonomically than ribs and vertebrae. Third, some bones tend to be more durable than others and thus preserve better. Given that nature and human activity could create a similar archaeological fish bone record, further tests are needed to better re-create the ancient Fayum fishing strategies. For example, those believing in the decapitation explanation need to find a site where vertebrae and ribs dominate the fish bone record, thereby validating the existence of two types of sites, one for fishing/processing and one for consuming. Thus far, this has not occurred. However, tests conducted on the mechanical breakdown of fish skeletal elements showed that fish vertebrae and ribs were among the first to be damaged to such a point that their identification was compromised. This would suggest that the archaeological pattern noted in the Fayum was not necessarily a by-product of human behavior.

POST-PROCESSUALISM

Processualism began to be critiqued soon after it emerged, largely by British archaeologists who, because Old World archaeology was more closely allied with the humanities, had never felt comfortable with their American counterparts' identification with anthropology. In particular, Michael Shanks, Christopher Tilley, and Ian Hodder took issue with processualism's environmental determinism, failure to take into account human individualism such as gender, ethnicity, and identity, and supposed objectivity of interpretation. Influenced by the broader movement of post-modernism, they argued for a subjective and relative view of the past and undertook to analyze not only the material remains they excavated, but also themselves, their attitudes, and their biases. Called post-processualism, this new model found favor with a diverse group of scholars, including feminists, neo-Marxists, and cognitive and contextual archaeologists, all of whom are united by their opposition to processualism.

Post-processualists believe that the entire scientific approach to archaeology is flawed, because we cannot possibly interpret archaeological phenomena without relying on our own cultural biases as part of that interpretation. That is, there is no reason to believe – and no way to prove – that our perception of the ancient world in any way matches the perception of the ancients themselves. Post-processualists state that personal biases inevitably affect the very questions archaeologists ask and direct them to the conclusions they are predisposed to believe. The essential difference between post-processualism and processualism can be captured in their fundamental views of archaeology: processual archaeologists attempt to construct an objective past whereas post-processualists believe that the past is what we create it to be.

For example, a processual archaeologist might attempt to describe the ancient Egyptian state as a functionally differentiated but integrated society where scores of occupational specialists, from farmers and bricklayers to judges and tax collectors, as well as a myriad of other occupations, depended on each other for goods and services. If the army did not receive its rations, then it could not defend against the "hordes" of intruders trying to cross Egypt's frontiers. If administrators did not store and redistribute goods collected through taxation, then those not involved in food production might starve. Thus, the poorest farmer and the king himself were linked in a mutually dependent, hierarchically arranged socioeconomic and political relationship. If one sector were to break down, the entire complex could falter or even collapse.

In contrast, a post-processualist would likely dismiss the very term "state" (or civilization) on the grounds that it imposes a sterile and untenable typology on Egyptian culture that presupposes its culturo-historic, transformative path through time. Rather, he or she would seek to analyze ancient Egypt not by the material remains and the techniques used to make them, but by detailed descriptions of the complex social and ideological contexts and activities through which the remains (i.e., artifacts) were originally created and used. Traditional archaeologists naturally question the soundness of basing explanations on inferences about ideologies and activities for which there are no mechanisms to substantiate or negate any derived conclusions.

Despite differences between the three approaches, there is common ground between them, and all make useful contributions to understanding the past. All are concerned about how we know about people in the past and whether that knowledge represents the actual past or just a personal mental reconstruction of the past. Good culture history is still the foundation for processual-type explanations – that is, the "what," "when," and "where" need to be answered before the questions of "how" and "why" can be framed. Even archaeologists who subscribe to post-processual theoretical frameworks rely on many techniques such as stratified sampling, statistics, and biochemical/material analysis that originated from the scientific, processual mind-set.

ARCHAEOLOGICAL TERMS

All archaeologists are interested in learning about past humans by examining the material culture they have left behind. Thus, the bases for all archaeological investigations are artifacts and features – broadly defined as anything that owes its physical characteristics or its location to human activity. A beautifully made Egyptian vase is an "artifact," as is a pile of stones used to mark the boundary of an ancient field, or a bone left over from an ancient meal. "Features" are non-portable artifacts. Examples include ancient fire hearths, storage pits, or even a linear mound of earth used to direct water. A grouping of artifacts and/or features is called a "site." To an archaeologist, both the great Temple of Karnak and a scatter of stone chips made by a Paleolithic hunter are sites, and both are worthy of investigation.

The myriad ways in which artifacts and features are collected and analyzed are known as archaeological "methods." Although excavation – the documentation and collecting of artifacts from controlled removal of earthen layers – is a hallmark of archaeology, it is expensive, time-consuming, and destructive, so it is undertaken sparingly. Other means for artifact study include the examination of museum collections, remote sensing using high-tech means to "view" subsurface materials, and site survey whereby surface collections are used as indicators of subsurface deposits. Determining the age of an artifact can also be done using a variety of methods such as seriation and radiocarbon dating.

When a method is applied to actual data, it is known as a "technique." This can be rather confusing to both archaeologists and non-archaeologists alike, as the distinction is not applied uniformly in the literature. Sometimes, the word "method" is taken to mean a general procedure whereas "technique" refers to a specific type of that procedure, as in "sampling" is a method and the various types of sampling – random, stratified, and so forth – are techniques. But in actuality, all archeological procedures, be they general or specific, are methods when they are spoken of as a concept and become techniques when they are applied in the real world. This separate use of the terms allows for the evaluation of both the actual method and its application in a specific instance. In other words, researchers need to be able to determine if errors can be introduced through the use of a faulty method or the misapplication of a good method (faulty technique).

When archaeologists move from data collection and analysis to the explanation or interpretation of relationships in the data, they utilize concepts from science such as law/principle, hypothesis, and theory. A scientific "law" or "principle" is a statement of fact about or a description of the natural world that is accepted to be true and universal (sometimes termed an axiom). As such, it is an initial premise, or assumption, on which further scientific arguments are based. Examples of laws of nature include the law of gravity, Newton's laws of motion, and the laws of thermodynamics. The geologic law of superposition – that older layers of earth lie beneath more recent layers – is the basis for much of archaeology.

A "hypothesis" is an *explanation* for a single phenomenon or event based on empirical observation. Hypotheses make predictions that can be supported or refuted by experimentation or continued observation. The use of hypotheses and hypothesis testing in archaeology comes out of the processual approach and its attempts to apply scientific rigor to archaeological research. Archaeologists use hypotheses to define problems for current and future research.

Although the term "hypothesis" is used fairly consistently in science, in popular discourse it is often confused with the word "theory." This has resulted partly from the fact that there is no standard definition for "theory" even among scientists, although there is consensus about what a theory consists of and what it should do. In its broadest sense, a theory is an overarching, comprehensive explanation of how nature works and why. Theories allow us to classify phenomena and understand relationships between these phenomena. Theories are well supported by many strands of empirical evidence, including observation and experimentation, and they are predictive. Additionally, theories are complex and dynamic, comprising both statements that are not falsifiable (laws/principles/axioms) and those that are (hypotheses). Sometimes theories are abandoned, but more often they are revised to conform to new observations by modifying the assertions made in the component hypotheses or by restricting the class of phenomena to which the theory applies.

Although some attempts have been made to develop archaeological theories, most notably regarding general explanations for the rise of agriculture and the growth of the state, most theories that archaeologists utilize come from other disciplines. Evolutionary theory, explicit or not, underlies much of archaeology's attempts to describe and explain changes in material culture. Additionally, much of the materialist approach of processual archaeology can be linked to earlier Marxist theory, whereas post-processual archaeology has been influenced by neo-Marxism and critical theory.

ARCHAEOLOGY IN EGYPT

Although most of our current knowledge of ancient Egypt's past, particularly the historical period, has been compiled by Egyptologists, there exist a tremendous number of cultural and historical problems that the application of archaeological methods and techniques could serve to elucidate. Anthropological archaeology has recently made inroads in studies of Egypt's prehistory. Because of the nature of prehistoric remains, generalizing anthropological questions such as how the domestication of animals, agriculture, the nation-state, and written language developed in Egypt and how that compares to other early cultures are best dealt with from an archaeological paradigm. The kinds of data, results, and interpretations that can be made through the complex, patchy, and sometimes quirky archaeological record differs from and often complements information gained through textual and art historical sources, and it is safe to say that the potential for archaeology in Egypt has yet to be fully realized.

In this book, I focus on the contributions made by archaeologists and the methods and techniques we use to gather and interpret information about Egypt's past. For the purposes of this text, archaeology will remain at the forefront of all discussions, but readers should be aware that scholars from numerous other backgrounds contribute to our understanding of ancient

Egypt. It is also important to remember that the interpretations that result from archeological studies are just that: archaeologists' interpretation of the data. We cannot "re-create" the past, but we can create models of increasing refinement that approximate the past in order to gain a better understanding of the human experience.

2

THE FIRST EGYPTIANS: THE ART AND SCIENCE OF DATING

Two of the most common lay questions posed to archaeologists presenting their Paleolithic findings are: "How do you know how old it is?" and "What was it used for?" In fact, these two basic questions embody the dual nature of modern archaeology as both a historical and scientific discipline. Problems of chronology – when this object was made, when that monument was destroyed, when these people were buried – are inherently historical and particularizing. Conversely, the answer to the second question focuses on archaeology's generalizing aspect. Obviously, no archaeologist is going to be able to give a definitive answer as to what task every artifact was employed to do, or precisely how old an artifact is, but through analogy and accepted practices embedded in comparative studies as well as scientific rigor, the age and ancient function of many artifacts can be reasonably determined.

A great deal of time and effort has been spent on constructing dating systems for ancient Egypt and, in fact, Egypt has arguably the most accurate and complete chronological framework of any ancient culture. Archaeologists working in the historical period, such as Egyptologists, rely heavily on the Egyptian dynastic chronology, one of the oldest and most reliable means of affixing a calendrical (or absolute) date to an object or site. Simply put, a historic object is dated by its association or similarity to artifacts known to correlate with a particular dynasty. The dating of Paleolithic materials, however, is neither so straightforward nor as accurate or reliable.

Paleolithic archaeology relies heavily on geology for much of its inferences about the past. Archaeology, geology, and paleontology have matured together as a discipline, but archaeology has probably benefited the most from its association with its sister disciplines. The age of recovered materials and the setting within which they are found often leave no alternative source for dating or understanding their past role except by reference to geological context.

Archaeological geology, or geoarchaeology, encompasses a large scope of endeavors, from evaluating the landscape of a site to better understand how

TABLE 2.1. *Nile evolution and geologic time*

Geologic time period	Nile phases	Date (BC)
Holocene	Nile	8,000
Upper Pleistocene	Neonile	30,000
Upper Pleistocene	Prenile	500,000–125,000
Middle Pleistocene	Protonile	600,000
Pliocene	Paleonile	3,000,000
Miocene	Eonile	5,000,000

the ancient inhabitants collected food, to studying stratigraphy for dating, analyzing sediments for the elucidation of site-forming processes, and reconstructing past environments through plant and animal remains. In essence it covers all geology-related problems as they relate to answering archaeological questions. For example, geologists have determined that the Nile is known to have gone through five distinct phases, each with different flow characteristics and each (except for the current one) transitioning through a period where no water flowed into Egypt from its current equatorial source (Table 2.1). Important to archaeology is the fact that each of the flow regimes left terraces that have been roughly dated and used to help estimate the age of some early artifacts. During this same span of time, today's deserts oscillated between extreme aridity and savanna-like conditions where seasonal lakes once served as gathering points for early humans. These sites, now deflated by arid winds, offer some of the oldest evidence for humans in Egypt. In some instances, such as in the Fayum, even the lack of sediments has lent itself to a better understanding of Egypt's past. Clearly, the study of sediments, in particular their layered arrangement or stratification, is a primary tool of the archaeologist.

RELATIVE DATING TECHNIQUES

The geological law of superposition, the guiding principle of sedimentology and thereby archaeological excavation, is one of Paleolithic archaeology's most important dating techniques. The law of superposition, simply put, states that a level or layer of earth is older than those that overlie it (Figure 2.1). That is, as we excavate deeper into the earth, we encounter older sediments and artifacts. With proper measurement of artifact location and record keeping, a scholar can mark the passage of time by noting which artifact was recovered from what stratagraphic layer and thereby create a relative chronology, meaning that a sequence of artifacts can be ordered from most recent to oldest. However, this does not allow us to fix precise calendrical (absolute) dates to the objects.

FIGURE 2.1. Stratigraphic sequence showing overlaying units at an excavation of an Early Dynastic Delta site. Note the thin light-colored layers of ash overlying the mudbrick, and in turn the mudbrick overlying the darker mixed sediments (photo by D. J. Brewer).

Seriation typology, previously called sequence dating, is another common means of establishing relative dates. This method involves noting how artifacts, particularly stone tools and pottery, change through time (Figure 2.2; a more detailed discussion of seriation in pottery follows in Chapter 4). Advances in manufacturing techniques as well as changes in style and artistic decoration often allow these objects to be ordered in a relative sequence. These objects then serve as time markers for associated artifacts and sediments. As with excavation, seriation does not give us exact dates for the objects but it does allow us to deduce where they fall in a sequence from earliest to latest.

Another commonly employed chronological method is cross-dating, which, like seriation, is rooted in the concept of typology. Cross-dating archaeological artifacts relies on the assumption that a dated artifact type at one archaeological site will be of the same approximate age when found elsewhere. Cross-dating has been shown to be reasonably accurate when based on relatively short-lived types, such as those in pottery, but more caution should be used when deriving chronologies from stone tools, as many types can persist for centuries or even millennia.

"ABSOLUTE" DATING METHODS

Although they are a reliable and essential archaeological tool, relative dating methods do not fully satisfy the archaeologist. Merely knowing that something is younger or older than something else is not enough. Since the mid-twentieth century, archaeologists have made use of developments in chemistry and physics to assign dates to artifacts by measuring radioactive decay or accumulation. Correlated to real (absolute) dates within a calculated standard deviation, these techniques are regarded as accurate, if not absolute. (Although these techniques are often described as "absolute" dating techniques in contrast to the relative dating techniques discussed above, it is more accurate to call them radiometric dating methods because they do not give us a real, calendrical date but rather a range of dates.) The most common of these methods are radiocarbon dating and luminescence dating; other methods include potassium-argon dating and electron-spin resonance.

Radiocarbon dating is based on the disintegration of the radioactive isotope carbon-14 (C-14). All living organisms absorb atmospheric carbon-14, so the level of C-14 in plants and animals when they die approximately equals the level of C-14 in the atmosphere at that time. After the organism dies, the unstable carbon-14 breaks down to become nitrogen-14 at a regular rate (the half-life). The amount of carbon-14 remaining in a once-living sample is thus a measure of time elapsed since the organism's death. There is, however, a finite amount of carbon-14 in any organism, and thus the technique has a dating limit of about 60,000 years, beyond which too few radioactive carbon-14 elements remain to make an accurate count. Any organic material can be tested, but the best, in order of reliability, are charcoal, wood, bone, shell, and horn.

Raw radiocarbon ages are reported in years "before present" (bp or BP), based on what was calculated to be the level of carbon-14 in 1950. (Thus, years "before present" really means years "before 1950.") These raw dates are also based on a slightly incorrect value for the radiocarbon half-life, but this value, which cancels itself out in the calculations, is used for consistency with earlier published dates. Raw radiocarbon dates are not identical to calendar dates, however, due to the fact that C-14 radiation levels have not been constant over time or place. Raw dates are converted to calendar dates by means of calibration curves based on samples independently dated by other methods, such as dendrochronology (to about 10,000 years ago) and cave deposits (to about 45,000 years ago). Uncalibrated radiocarbon ages are often reported

FIGURE 2.2. Predynastic and Early Dynastic vessels illustrating the evolution of wavy-handle decoration through time. Note how the handle changes from a raised band to a thin line encircling the vessel and finally disappears (Courtesy of the Oriental Institute of the University of Chicago).

with a lower case (bp) or RCYBP (radiocarbon years before present), whereas calibrated dates are reported as uppercase (BP or cal BP).

Radiocarbon dating laboratories also report an uncertainty for each date. For example, 7500 BP +/− 100 indicates a statistical standard deviation of 100 radiocarbon years. In other words, there is a 66 percent chance that the real date of the artifact falls somewhere in the range of 7600–7400 BP. The older or poorer the sample is, the larger the error factor (i.e., +/− a larger number). Because dates are based on statistical (parametric) averages and thus only have a 66 percent chance of being correct, it is important to retrieve more than one sample from a given strata or object for testing. A date's accuracy can also be affected by lab techniques, quality of the archaeological sample, and the method of calibrating the laboratory date to compensate for the age of the sample and its geographic area of origin.

In addition, other factors can make interpreting radiocarbon dates less than straightforward. For example, a colleague and close friend was involved in a project to date the pyramids using carbon samples taken from the mortar between the huge blocks of stone. One afternoon he relayed to me in utter despair that the C-14 dates were not only 400 years older than other evidence suggested, but they also indicated that the pyramids were built from the top down as the oldest dates came from the highest levels and the youngest dates from the lower courses! Clearly other factors were involved. A re-running of the samples did correct for the "upside-down" nature of the original C-14 dates, but the incident serves as cautionary lesson: No single dating technique is an infallible resource.

Another dating technique applied in Egypt is luminescence dating, which is based on the measurement of the amount of light that is released upon thermal (TL) or optical stimulation (OSL) dating of samples containing crystalline minerals such as quartz and feldspar. The light signal is a measure of the radiation dose that has accumulated since the material was either heated (ceramics, lava) or exposed to sunlight (sediments). Some of the energy of this radiation is stored in the form of trapped electrons; when the crystalline material is re-exposed to heat or light in the laboratory, the trapped electrons escape and give off a weak light signal, or luminescence. Thermal luminescence has been used for over forty years to date heated materials such as potsherds, volcanic glass, burnt stone tools, and burnt sediments, while the more recent OSL has been used to date unheated sediments that were exposed to sunlight before they were buried, such as certain wind- or water-borne deposits. The great advantage that luminescence dating has over radiocarbon dating is its ability to date nonorganic material over a fairly wide age range (from a few hundred years ago to around 200,000 years ago).

As with the C-14 pyramid example, all dating methods have their strengths and weaknesses, and it is dangerous to rely solely on a single method. More reliable results can be achieved using multiple methods.

DATING THE PALEOLITHIC PERIOD: STONE TOOL TYPOLOGIES

Because many of Egypt's earliest sites are found on or near the desert's surface, neither stratigraphy nor carbon dating is applicable. Thus, dating the earliest periods of Egyptian prehistory often relies on one of the oldest and least precise of archaeological methods: stone tool typologies and cross-dating. As elsewhere, Egypt's Paleolithic Period is divided into three main periods: Lower, Middle and Upper Paleolithic, each with a set of characteristic stone tools used to both identify and date the ancient sites (Table 2.2).

Archaeologists refer to three main classes of stone tools when establishing their chronologies: cores, flakes, and blades. Early pebble tools, hand axes, choppers, and cleavers are considered types of core tools (Figure 2.3a). In each case the working tool is what is left of the stone once the flakes have been removed (knapped). A core also refers to the prepared nucleus of a stone from which flakes have been removed to create flake tools (Figure 2.3b). Removal of

TABLE 2.2. *Upper, middle, lower Paleolithic industries of Egypt*

Date	Industry	Egyptian variant
5,000 BC	Neolithic	
		Qarunian
		Shamarkian
6,500 BC	Epipaleolithic	
		Arkinians
		Qadan
		Halfan
		Kubbaniyan
		Idfuan
20,000 BC	Upper Paleolithic	
		Khormusan
		Aterian
		Mousterian
90,000 BC	Middle Paleolithic	
		Arkin 8
		Umm Shagir
		Bir Sahara-14
300,000 BC	Lower Paleolithic	

(a)   (b)

FIGURE 2.3. An Acheulian hand ax – a core tool (a) and a Mousterian core (b) from which flakes were created to make the smaller, more refined tools of the Levallois technique (photo courtesy of the Spurlock Museum, University of Illinois).

a flake from a core leaves a scar on both the core and the flake, which can help identify aspects of the tool manufacture process. A skilled knapper can create flakes in different sizes and dimensions depending on the material makeup of the percussion instrument (antler, wood, stone) and the power of the strike directed at the core, the ultimate goal being a flake or blade with the best properties for use in creating a specific tool such as a knife, scraper, or even projectile point. (A blade is simply a flake with parallel sides, struck from a specially prepared core to be later modified into a special-purpose tool.)

Archaeologists refer to Paleolithic stone tools by industry and function. The term "industry" usually applies to the tool's manufacturing technique and often will take its name from the first site at which such tools were discovered (a naming system much like Egypt's Predynastic cultural sequence). For example, the Acheulean industry was initially found at Saint-Acheul in France and has given its name to the industry and its distinctive hand axes.

Stone tools are further classified by their inferred function, such as choppers, scrapers, or grinders. Once a name and function has been identified, these properties carry through to other occurrences of similar tools. Following this rule, an Acheulean hand ax discovered in Egypt dates to and was used for similar purposes as those found in France. This creates a circular type of argument whereby a tool can be dated by the site, or a site can be dated by the tool type – a practice proven to be in error on more than one occasion when dating Egyptian sites by reference to a European-based chronology.

The earliest stone tool industry in Africa is associated with *Homo habilis* and called the Oldowan. The tools were simple river pebbles from which a few flakes were knocked off to make a working edge (Figure 2.4); these represent the total sum of human technology for almost a million years. There remains some debate, however, as to whether the Oldowan is present in Egypt. A trio of scholars believes that sharpened river pebbles recovered from deeply embedded geological strata near ancient Thebes (ca. 1.5 million years BC) belong to the Oldowan industry. Unfortunately, these tools, which were nothing more than simple nodules with a few flakes removed (creating a sharp working edge), have never been made available for scholarly study. Thus the presence in Egypt of *Homo habilis* and the Oldowan industry awaits verification.

LOWER PALEOLITHIC TYPOLOGIES

Although the presence of the Oldowan in Egypt is a matter of debate, there is little disagreement surrounding the Acheulean period and its presumed

FIGURE 2.4. A simple pebble tool of the type associated with *Homo habilis* (courtesy of Didier Descouens).

creator, *Homo erectus*. Egypt's Lower Paleolithic Acheulean industry is best identified by the pear-shaped (sometimes oval) Acheulean hand ax: a stone that was basically chipped on both sides, creating a type of ax or cleaver for chopping and cutting. The unmodified flakes coming off the stone core were also used for cutting. Tools identified as Acheulean have been found from Cairo to Khartoum; one of the oldest was recovered across the river from the great statues of Ramesses II at Abu Simbel. This find, a hand ax, was dated by geological association to sediments laid down by the river some 700,000 years ago. Although the exact date of individual finds based on geological strata might be questioned, work on later sites in the Western Desert provides unambiguous evidence for the presence of Acheulean peoples in Egypt at 300,000 BC.

When Lower Paleolithic Egyptians roamed North Africa, a moister, rainier period prevailed (Figure 2.5) and the Protonile, the river flowing through Egypt at this time, was a braided, intertwined network of river channels rather than a single channel, like today's Nile. Bones of giraffes, gazelles,

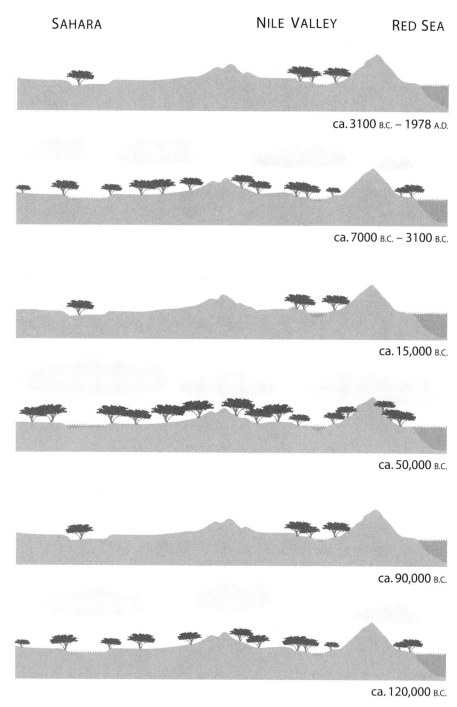

SAHARA   NILE VALLEY   RED SEA

ca. 3100 B.C. – 1978 A.D.

ca. 7000 B.C. – 3100 B.C.

ca. 15,000 B.C.

ca. 50,000 B.C.

ca. 90,000 B.C.

ca. 120,000 B.C.

FIGURE 2.5. At times in the geologic past, today's desert offered savanna-like conditions and was inhabited by numerous cultures (Brenda Coelho after Hoffman 1984, fig. 5).

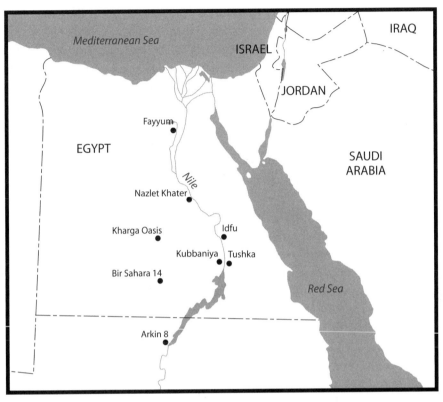

FIGURE 2.6. The approximate site location of the Paleolithic cultures discussed in the text (Ault and Flores).

and even elephants have been found dating to this period, indicating that a savanna-type fauna once covered these now-desert lands. To support these animals Egypt had to have received more rainfall than today, the result being a landscape probably looking more like the Serengeti Plain than the vast desolate deserts of our modern era. Geological evidence collected from wadis and lacustrine (lake or pond) deposits suggest, however, that these were not lush, year-round grasslands but rather seasonal savannas marked by an annual moist period. Because waterholes were sparse and separated by vast areas of arid land, migration out onto the savannas most likely occurred during the rainy season. During the dry season the area's inhabitants would have retreated to oases and other permanent sources of water.

One of the most important Acheulean period sites in Egypt is Arkin 8, (Figure 2.6) discovered by the Polish archaeologist Waldemar Chmielewski near the modern Sudan–Egypt border. Arkin 8 artifacts were predominantly pebble tools, dating the site to the Lower Paleolithic Period. Because the artifact concentrations appeared to shift across the site, it was determined to be a temporary camp visited on a regular, possibly seasonal, basis over many years. As with most Paleolithic sites in Egypt, Arkin 8 was not particularly well preserved but it did contain an astonishingly large number of artifacts (over 3,400) for a site of this age, including the remains of an early structure thought to date to about 100,000 BC. Composed of a series of sandstone blocks arranged in a semicircle with an oval-shaped foundation (1.8 meters by 1.2 meters) dug some 30 centimeters deep, it probably represents one of the earliest human structures in the world.

Another Lower Paleolithic site, also located deep in the desert, is Bir Sahara-14 (ca. 100,000+ BC), which lies around an ancient spring (Figure 2.6). During the Lower Paleolithic Period, a number of artesian springs arose from a sandstone formation lying 18 meters below the desert surface, and these springs created numerous oases across the desert. Now only a few, such as Kharga, remain. At Bir Sahara-14, 113 Late Acheulean tools were recovered, although none of the famous hand axes were part of the inventory. Perhaps more important was the recovery of animal bones representing several large ruminants, an equid (probably ass), and warthog, all of which reinforce the notion that the area possessed savanna-like conditions.

Although Lower Paleolithic sites such as Bir Sahara-14 and Arkin 8 do reveal important information about Egypt's earliest inhabitants, they cannot be precisely dated because they extend beyond the 50,000 to 70,000–year limit of the carbon-14 dating method. Furthermore, because they are surface sites, we cannot date them using geology. Thus, we can offer only approximate dates based on the style and sophistication of the stone tools, which has led to some scholarly debates over their age.

MIDDLE PALEOLITHIC TYPOLOGIES

About 90,000 years ago, the rains that characterized the Lower Paleolithic Period ended, and the Sahara became a vast, hyperarid desert. During this dry spell, it is assumed that the peoples inhabiting the Sahara took refuge in the Nile Valley and the great oases, such as Kharga. It was at this time that a more efficient stone tool industry developed, the Levalloisian, named after the site in France where it was first identified. This new technique employed flakes to make the tools, the flakes having been created by striking a prepared core. Simply put, Acheulean tools were made by chipping flakes off a stone, with the remaining stone core becoming the tool (Figure 2.7). In the Middle Paleolithic Period, the stone core (Figure 2.7) provided the raw material and

ACHEULEAN

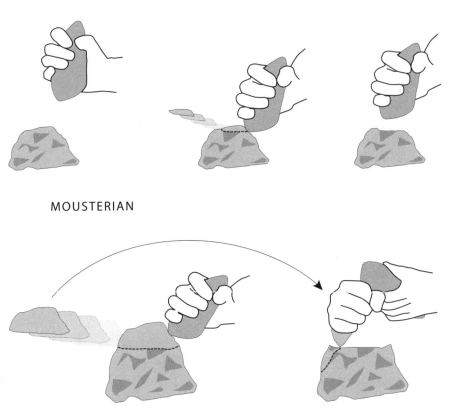

MOUSTERIAN

FIGURE 2.7. Acheulean tools were made by chipping flakes off a stone, with the remaining stone core becoming the tool (see Fig. 2.3a). In the later Levallois technique, the stone core provided the raw material and the flakes became the tool, with many tools made from one stone (see Fig. 2.3b). Because the core was specially prepared for flaking, each flake could be made thin and symmetrical, which meant more and different types of tools could be made from a single stone than by using the previous Acheulean technique (Loren Kirkwood after Brewer 2005, fig. 4.4).

the flakes became the tool (see Figure 2.3). Because the core was specially prepared for flaking via the Levallois technique, more and different types of tools could be made from the flakes of a single stone than in the previous Acheulean industry, most notably the spear point.

Levallois points were not only more effective than the hardened wood and stone points that came before them, but they were fashioned to be hafted to a shaft. This offered an opportunity to hunt different types of animals and to hunt them more effectively. It was also at about this time that a moist, rainier

FIGURE 2.8. Classic "tanged" Aterian point (Courtesy of Josef Elwanger).

climate returned to the region. Springs, lakes, and lush grasslands covered much of the Sahara, even surpassing the seasonal savanna conditions that had prevailed in the earlier Lower Paleolithic Period.

Whether technological innovation and the onset of a more hospitable climate were connected or just coincidental is not certain, but thanks to these factors (and also others we will probably never know), a true flowering of cultures occurred in the Middle Paleolithic Period, and artifacts have been found from the Red Sea to Libya. In fact, some areas of the desert are literally carpeted with Middle Paleolithic tools.

Two new industries emerge during this time, the Aterian and the Khormusan; they offer a prime example of the limitations of archaeology when dates are based on lithic tool typologies and explanations are based on samples of tools that may or may not accurately represent all the activities and peoples that created them. The Aterian Industry, named for the type site at Bir el-Ater in Tunisia, began sometime around 40,000 BC and ended around 30,000 BC. Perhaps the most identifiable artifact of the culture was its characteristic projectile point. Aterian points are characterized by a distinct "tang" at their base, which allowed them to be fitted more securely to a spear or dart shaft (Figure 2.8).

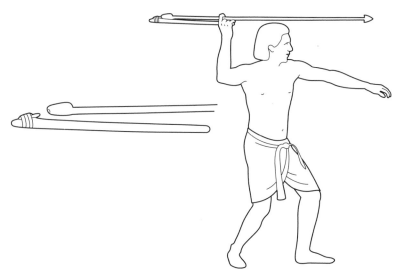

FIGURE 2.9. Aterian technology: The dart, a stone point affixed to a light shaft, is propelled with greater force when aided by a specially designed throwing stick (by Loren Kirkwood after Brewer 2005, fig. 4.6).

The dart was meant to be hurled via a throwing stick (Figure 2.9). It was the big game rifle of its time, with the vast increase in number and type of animal bones recovered from Aterian sites being evidence of its effectiveness. Faunal remains reported from Aterian sites include a large extinct aurochsen (cow), two species of gazelle, antelopes of different sizes, wild ass, fox, jackal, warthog, ostrich, turtle, and birds.

Interestingly, the Aterians, with their sophisticated tools and hunting prowess, lived side by side with other peoples who used simpler tools and lacked the finely made dart points. Some sites are separated by a mere 14 kilometers. At about the same time that Aterians and the other Mousterian cultures were prevalent in the Western Desert (40,000–33,000 BP), people referred to as Khormusans were living along the river. Like Aterians, Khormusans appear to have been hunters, but they were also good fishers. Because Khormusans crafted and used a particular tool known as a burin (Figure 2.10), they were mistakenly thought, like European burin users, to be Upper Paleolithic in age. Radiocarbon dates, however, show them to be Middle Paleolithic, suggesting early Egyptians were using burin tools much earlier than ancient Europeans, and reinforcing the fact that European chronologies should be viewed with caution when applied to Egyptian artifacts.

In an attempt to simplify the cultural landscape of Middle Paleolithic Egypt, some scholars prefer to order these groups into a sequence from Mousterian to Aterian, culminating with the Khormusan. There are some, however, who believe these groups to be contemporary, suggesting that food was plentiful enough to allow very different cultures to live amicably and successfully on the Saharan savannas. Yet others feel some of these industries might represent the same group of people carrying out different tasks in different places and, therefore, used different kinds of tools. The underlying issue is that we simply do not have a large enough sample of tools from different sites across different areas of Egypt to be sure which of these explanations is correct. What radiocarbon dates are available do not settle the argument in that they suggest that these groups overlapped for many thousands of years (see Table 2.2). Currently we might propose that as long as the Sahara remained hospitable, we can surmise that Mousterians, Aterians, Khormusans, and probably many other groups prospered and lived side by side, or we have divided the tools of a single group into separate, discrete industries based on insufficient data.

Although the array of lithic tools and imprecise dating remains a frustrating problem, for the curious there is one very interesting discovery about this period that has received relatively little attention: We have our first look at a Paleolithic ancient Egyptian. Associated with geological levels that produced Levalloisian tools, the skeleton of an immature Middle Paleolithic human was recovered: the earliest known human remains from Egypt. Although across Europe the Middle Paleolithic Period is associated with Neanderthals, there is as yet no conclusive evidence to substantiate their presence in Egypt. Unfortunately, this burial and its remains were poorly preserved but we do know that the individual was not fully grown, and what is important is that he or she was an anatomically modern human, not a Neanderthal.

UPPER PALEOLITHIC TYPOLOGIES

By 37,000 BC evidence suggests that the area was slowly becoming more arid such that by the beginning of the Upper Paleolithic Period (ca. 30,000 BC), deserts once again dominated the Egyptian landscape. Even the great Kharga Oasis apparently disappeared and was abandoned for nearly 20,000 years. What happened to the Aterian and Mousterian peoples? To be sure many groups probably perished, but some likely gravitated to the Nile. The Nile Valley served as a refuge and a melting pot of Middle Paleolithic culture. It is under these conditions that Nazlet Khater, one of the oldest Upper Paleolithic sites in Egypt, was occupied. The site, which was apparently a source of stone for tool making, dates to an arid period (ca. 32,000–29,500 BC) when Egypt probably looked similar to today.

FIGURE 2.10. The burin, thought to be an engraving type tool that could be re-sharpened with a skillfully placed blow directed behind the point (arrow) (Ault and Flores after Wendorf and Schild 1975, fig. 7).

The ancient visitors of Nazlet Khater excavated several shafts and underground chambers to retrieve chert cobbles from an ancient Nile river terrace. It is here that an important technological development is first noted in Egypt: the creation of lithic blades. Blades are simply long slender flakes struck off a prepared core and used to make a variety of tools. It is also here that the second earliest human so far discovered in Egypt was found. This individual was an adult male. He was buried lying on his back with his head turned to the west. A bifacial ax had been placed near his face – the earliest attested funerary gift in Egypt. A second skeleton was found 30 meters away along with remains of a fetus, but the bones were so poorly preserved that nothing is known of this individual. They do appear, however, to be anatomically modern humans although some suggestion of archaic features, such as an overly thick mandible, has been reported.

Based on geological evidence such as Nile and desert sediments, as well as plant and animal fossils, archaeologists believe a moister, more hospitable climate than that of today returned to Egypt from about 17,000 to 14,000 BC. It is at this time that newly adapted river-oriented cultures appear along the Nile possessing a technology that surpassed the earlier Khormusans. What set these groups apart was their use of microblades. Microblades were merely tiny blades prepared as blanks for fashioning tools at a later time, but because the preferred flint was available only in small nodules, a "micro"-lithic tradition evolved that made the most parsimonious use of the resource.

We have evidence that at least three microlithic groups flourished in Upper Egypt between about 17,000 and 15,000 BC: the Kubbaniyan, the Idfuan, and the Qadan.

The Kubbaniyans, whose sites date to about 16,070–15,640 BC, divided their time between two distinct but overlapping habitats. During the winter and spring (November to July), they camped on the borderlands between the dune fields and the floodplain of the Nile – a position that enabled them to exploit both the riverine fish and any grazing animals that might range into the hinterlands after a rare winter shower. When the Nile floodplain's annual inundation began in late June, the Kubbaniyans retreated farther back into the dunes to avoid the floodwaters. There they camped and exploited the fish trapped in pools left by the receding flood and hunted any game animals that fed or sheltered in the mini-oases created by the pooled floodwater (Figure 2.11).

There is evidence that along with hunting, fishing, and collecting plants for immediate consumption, Kubbaniyans were also storing food. This marks another important milestone in Egyptian history. Storing food requires important decisions to be made and on a frequent basis. A critical issue at Kubbaniya is that the amount of stored foodstuffs went beyond the needs of a single family. In other words, it was community-based storage, which requires a decision maker to work on behalf of a group larger than the immediate family. First, someone has to decide that storing surplus food for the benefit of the community is a beneficial strategy. Second, someone has to determine what food and how much to store. Surplus foods then need to be collected and facilities constructed for storage. Third, these facilities must be protected from pests as well as the potential human robber. Under these circumstances the first step in building a hierarchy of community decision makers has begun.

Around 12,000 BC a major climatic event occurred: Nile floods reached abnormally high levels, averaging some eight to nine meters above the modern flood plain, followed (ca. 9500 BC) by a period of hyper-aridity and low Nile floods. Few sites have been recovered from this time period. Some archaeologists believe that because the area's occupants would have followed the Nile to its new, lower-level shores, these occupations are now buried under meters of silt deposited by later Nile floods. Others, however, believe that the stress placed on the valley dwellers was such that it was easier to make a living elsewhere and the valley was simply abandoned.

Nevertheless, archaeologists have discovered three cemeteries dating to this time period (13000–9000 BC), and with this discovery are able for the first

winter

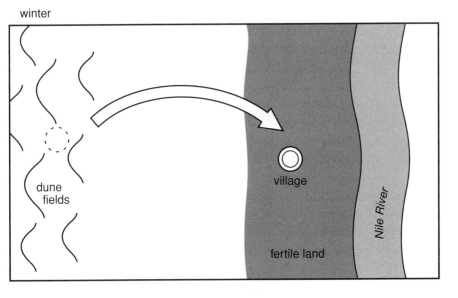

summer

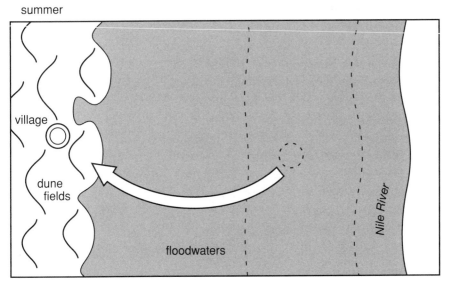

FIGURE 2.11. Kubbaniyans moved seasonally between the border area of the Nile's fertile black soil and desert to the desert swales (small dunes) (by Loren Kirkwood after Brewer 2005, fig. 4.8).

time to satisfy our curiosity not only about what these ancient people looked like, but about how they lived and perhaps something about their beliefs. Obviously cemetery sites are very important to archaeologists because of the diverse types of information that we can obtain from the study of graves and skeletons. Analysis of the skeletal remains provides information about physical stature and diet, and the diseases that plagued these early Egyptians, as well as longevity and quality of life. Studying the grave itself can provide important information about social class and religious beliefs.

A total of fifty-nine skeletons of men, women, and children were recovered from one cemetery, believed to be around 12,000 years old and attributed to the Qadan culture. The bodies were buried loosely flexed on their left sides with their heads directed to the east. Often more than one individual shared the same grave (Figure 2.12), which in general were shallow oval pits covered by flat slabs of limestone. The skeletal remains show that Qadans were short by today's standards and slight of build. There is evidence they were plagued by familiar physical ailments such as arthritis, sacroiliac problems, osteitis, and possibly spinal tuberculosis, as well as a variety of dental disorders, including missing teeth, cavities, and abscesses.

Although the poor state of preservation and small number of individuals recovered make it difficult to draw precise conclusions, burials from this one Qadan site revealed rather unexpected discoveries. First, the people buried there constitute what can be called a representative population: Unlike most ancient cemeteries, which are usually dominated by the very young and very old, people of all ages were interred. A second and most unusual feature of the burials was the placement of 110 stone artifacts in positions that suggest they had penetrated the bodies as either arrow or spear points. Indeed, several lithics were found still imbedded in the bones. In the majority of cases, however, the stone artifacts were found along the vertebral column or in the chest cavity, lower abdomen, arms, and skull, suggesting that they had penetrated the soft tissues. In all, more than twenty-four individuals were associated with these small flake objects, with women and children accounting for half of these burials. Four persons had apparently suffered multiple wounds, and one grave yielded eight bodies that had been buried together. Fractured forearms and deep cut marks on the leg bones give further testimony to the nature of their deaths.

The obvious conclusion to be drawn from this evidence is that the Qadanians met a violent death – but why? What could have caused 40 percent of the interred individuals to die violently? One possible reason could be conflict caused by a reduction in the food supply, brought on by excessive Nile floods followed by hyper-aridity. With people of different groups and backgrounds moving into the Nile Valley, equally affected by the varying climate and loss of resources, territory might have become an issue, and the combination of

FIGURE 2.12. Qadan burials as they were unearthed by archaeologists during the UNESCO-sponsored Nubian Monuments campaign (courtesy of the Wendforf archives, © Trusties of the British Museum).

limited food resources and increased territoriality might have sparked competition and eventually conflict between peoples.

Finding the true reason behind the violent deaths of the Qadan people requires the ability to date the recovered skeletons precisely. For example, if these people were interred over a couple of centuries (the degree of error in any carbon-14 date of this age), then the number of deaths by violence would not be so dramatic. If, however, the bodies were interred as the result of a single episode or a series of repeated episodes over a short period of time, some specific issue or event clearly stimulated the violent interchange.

Interestingly, a Qadan cemetery located directly across the Nile and dating to about the same time period revealed little evidence of violence. Of the thirty-nine skeletons recovered, only two showed any sign of violent trauma. These folks were buried in a loosely flexed position but were not oriented in any particular way, suggesting perhaps a different cultural affinity. Here we

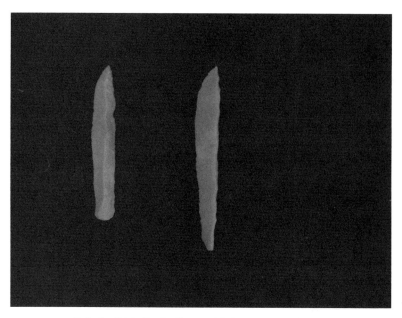

FIGURE 2.13. Epipaleolithic "backed" microblades. Note the delicately flaked back (right side) of each blade, which has been worked to protect the user from cutting his or her finger when applying downward pressure on the flint (photo by D. J. Brewer).

must remember that "Qadan" is identified by its lithic industry, which any number of cultural groups might possess.

At a third cemetery near Tushka, a few graves were marked by the horns of giant wild cattle (*Bos primigenious*), a custom reminiscent of later Early Dynastic royal graves, but again there is little evidence of violence. As there is no precise date for these cemeteries and they are now under the waters of Lake Nasser, little opportunity remains for solving this mystery.

The final thousand years of the Upper Paleolithic Period in Egypt is called the Epipaleolithic. The Nile Valley site of El-Kab reveals a full stratigraphic sequence of Epipaleolithic life: The lowest Epipaleolithic occupation level was carbon-14 dated to circa 6400 BC, a middle level to 6040 BC, and the upper level to 5980 BC. More than 4,000 artifacts were recovered, most of which were tiny, well-made microlithic tools such as burins and minutely retouched blades; the small blades were often backed to prevent the user from cutting his or her finger when using the tool (Figure 2.13). Ostrich eggshell beads were also common, indicating that people wore ornamentation. Because the sites have yielded many fish bones and were located close to the river, they could only have been occupied during low-water stages. Thus, they most likely represented seasonal fishing sites.

One of the most intriguing mysteries of prehistoric Egypt is the transition from Paleolithic to Neolithic life: The transformation from hunting and gathering to sedentary farming. We know very little about how and why this change occurred in Egypt. Perhaps nowhere is this cultural transition more accessible than in the Fayum depression. Not only was there a vibrant Epipaleolithic culture living along the shores of the lake, but some of the earliest Neolithic dates have been recovered here as well. But even here, the "why" and "how" of the transition from hunting and gathering to a sedentary agricultural way of life remain difficult to decipher.

Today the Fayum and its lake, Birket Qarun, lie about forty-four meters below sea level. The lake is extremely saline and essentially void of any indigenous animal life. During the Epipaleolithic Period, however, the lake was connected to the Nile by a natural channel that replenished its waters every year during the annual flood. Along the lake's shores and in the surrounding marshes, groups of people belonging to the Epipaleolithic Qarunian or Fayum B culture thrived. The area was home to a variety of fish and waterfowl, and wild animals watered there as well. Qarunian sites, dating from about 6240 to 5480 BC, can be found all along the old lake shoreline. These sites appear to be campsites, often with remains of fish and animals strewn about the hearths. Qarunian tools were small-backed blades and bladelettes of the microlithic tradition. With the onset of lower Nile floods beginning about 5480 BC, the lake's water was no longer replenished, the flood height having fallen below the elevation of the channel feeding the lake. When the lake disappeared, the Qarunian culture disappeared as well: Archaeologists have found no evidence of any occupation of the Fayum basin for nearly 300 years, after which a fully Neolithic people occupied the shorelines of the revitalized lake. These people raised domestic animals and plants and resembled in many ways the early agricultural groups developing at this time in the Nile Delta.

3

AGRICULTURE AND THE NILE VALLEY: BIOLOGY, THE ENVIRONMENT, AND SAMPLING

One of the most intriguing questions for archaeologists is the transition from Paleolithic to Neolithic life. Sometime around 7500–5000 BC, people in different parts of Egypt began shifting from a life based on hunting animals and gathering plants to one based on growing crops and raising livestock. This period, called the Neolithic ("New Stone Age"), occurs at roughly the same time across many parts of the world, and it has been accurately characterized as a revolution. It was this economic shift to food production that enabled people like the ancient Egyptians to amass great surpluses of food, which in turn permitted increases in population, craft specialization, and the construction of monumental public works. In fact, some scholars argue that agriculture has had a greater impact on human history than any other development.

Determining the causes of Egypt's shift to agriculture, however, has remained elusive. Debates arise between proponents of environmental, biological, or cultural explanations for agriculture's origins. After almost a century of rhetoric, the problem remains unresolved with no simple cause-and-effect relationship rising above another. Rather, as with so much of our human history, change – even change in a similar direction in different parts of the world – is shaped by local environmental and cultural conditions.

The peculiarity surrounding Egypt's transition to agriculture is that the earliest Neolithic sites studied seem already to have fully adopted an agricultural way of life, with plants and animals already clearly domesticated. There as yet does not seem to be a defined transitional period to the Neolithic, and seeking this evidence remains a priority for many archaeologists.

The process of domestication should not be confused with agriculture. Domestication refers to the biological changes of a species brought about through human interference in its normal environment, whereas agriculture is the process of increasing production of that species. The key concept in agriculture is human efforts to modify the environment of plants and animals to increase productivity: weeding gardens, penning pigs, running water ditches down seed rows. Although these activities may in the long run affect species biology, they are carried out to increase its production.

The most important clues to Egypt's shift to agriculture – the ancient plants and animals themselves – have proven to be controversial sources of information, and in some cases have actually fueled debate rather than solved any mystery. Plant and animal remains recovered through archaeological investigations are identified by specialists (paleobotanists and zooarchaeologists), who visually compare the archaeological specimens to known wild and domestic examples: a difficult task when working with seeds, plant, and bone fragments that have been subjected to thousands of years of aridity, erosion, and, in some cases, fossilization.

Most recently molecular studies have been directed at answering the question of whether a recovered plant or animal fragment is from a domesticate, but even these investigations have produced debatable results. Regardless of approach, determining whether a specimen is from an early domesticate is almost impossible because domestication is based on genetic changes that may or may not be reflected in the physical appearance of the plant or animal, and under these circumstances, one can never be sure what a molecular difference really represents.

When humans domesticate a plant or animal, they do so by interfering with the normal life cycle of that species. Domestication is not an event but a process, and over generations of intense exploitation of a wild form, it slowly becomes more dependent on human interference for its survival, to a point where it becomes totally dependent on people for some part of or all of its life cycle. In essence, what has happened biologically is that domestic plants and animals have adapted to conditions created by humans, which at the same time have made them less fit to survive on their own in the wild. One could even say that this is a co-evolutionary process in that both humans and the wild species begin to rely more and more on each other for survival. For example, because the connective stem holding the grain to the stock (the rachis) in domestic wheat (Figure 3.1) is tough and not brittle, it does not disperse easily from the headstock and has to be threshed. This trait is beneficial to humans because the seeds do not break from the headstock when harvested. However, it is a disadvantage to the plant if left to its own devices because its seeds cannot be dispersed by the wind or passing animals, thereby diminishing its chances of natural reproduction. Similarly, a domestic cow being grazed in a desert oasis would have difficulty fending for itself if its human caretakers were suddenly unavailable to assist its move to a new oasis for pasturage.

Plants and animals at either end of the wild-to-domestic spectrum usually can be classified with some certainty, but those in the process of being domesticated are hard to identify. Consequently, claims for early domestication and agriculture rely on other, more unequivocal, types of evidence such as:

* assessing the ecological fitness of a plant or animal vis-à-vis the local environment; that is, determining whether the organism could live in that area without the aid of humans;
* studying the artifacts found in association with the remains, particularly with regard to their use as agricultural tools; and
* identifying artistic renditions of plants and animals that are depicted in domesticated contexts.

With respect to ancient Egypt, the wild progenitors of wheat, sheep, and goat (and questionably, cattle and barley), which formed the backbone of its domestic economy, were not indigenous. Rather, they were introduced into Egypt from southwest Asia. Most archaeologists believe, therefore, that Paleolithic Egyptians learned agriculture from neighboring peoples, thereby shortening the time period for the development of an agricultural economy.

EGYPT AND THE EARLY NEOLITHIC

Where might we find evidence for the transitional phase to the Egyptian Neolithic? One of the first issues to ponder is the very question itself: Are we really asking the right question and, if so, what would the answer look like? Most archaeologists would argue that understanding one of the most important shifts in Egyptian history is what we as a discipline should be exploring and seeking to understand. The answer to our question, however, or at least its archaeological manifestation, might not look like what we expected to find. Searching for a transitional site or period that provides the "ah-ha" moment of discovery might not exist. That is, there may be no single site where we could definitively claim that here is where domestication or agriculture began in Egypt. Like the search for the missing fossil–link to our human ancestry, the path to agriculture and domestication was a process extending over a millennium, and therefore would be understandable only from a regional perspective, viewed across a large swath of time.

For example, by organizing the early Neolithic sites chronologically (oldest to youngest) a path from west of the Nile to east develops. Even recognizing

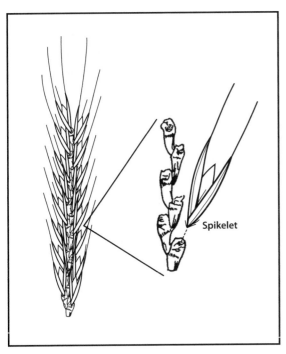

FIGURE 3.1. The connective stem or rachis (right) for wheat grains (Ault and Flores after Brewer et al. 1994, figure 3.2).

that we may not have a representative sample of all the important types of sites across this pathway, the correlation remains intriguing (Figure 3.2).

The earliest sites, located at Nabta (7500–7000 BC), produced grinding stones and some of the earliest examples of pottery in Egypt. One site in particular provided evidence that it was a long-term occupation, perhaps visited seasonally over a number of years. Evidence of a deep well, constructed with a set of stairs, shelters, or dwellings organized along paths, and communal storage pits and silos at the site represent common features of a society accustomed to residential stability. That plants, seeds, or grains were collected (and surpluses presumably stored) is supported by the discovery of mortars and pestles. The recovery of aurochsen bones (*Bos* spp.) of a similar size to known domesticates is a possible indicator of a pastoral society. Evidence compiled from modern pastoralist societies with communal storage facilities shows that someone had to decide what and how much to store, and later who receives the rations and how much.

The combined evidence is, however, only suggestive of a domestic economy, not conclusive. For example, the early Western Desert culture does not seem to have adopted the important element of sedentism: The large, socially organized desert site seems only to have been seasonally occupied. Rather, the sites show that ancient inhabitants seem to have maintained a mobile lifestyle, perhaps adding pastoralism and seasonal plant gathering to its varied resources. Even the presence of pastoralism is based on assumptions of biology (a reduction in animal size), which cannot always be attributed to human interference.

To the north and east of Nabta, regional surveys and site-specific analyses in the Fayum have provided archaeologists with enough information to gain a fairly good understanding of the ancient peoples that once occupied the area.

Indeed, like the Western Desert cultures, the Fayum cultures never seem to be fully sedentary, although two sites (Kom K and Kom W), like the large Nabta village site, were inhabited on a seasonal or long-term basis. It seems the Fayum still adhered to a seasonally exploitive way of life with all or at least part of the population moving to take advantage of seasonally available foodstuffs. As did the slightly earlier and contemporary cultures of the Sahara, they built communal storage pits for both grain and utensils. A detailed study of recovered fish fauna (in particular growth rings of the Nile catfish), reinforces the impression that Neolithic Fayum peoples followed the same seasonal strategies as their Epipaleolithic predecessors exploiting fish and other resources in similar relative abundances and at the same time of year.

Kozlowski and Ginter believe the Fayum Neolithic originated not from one but two sources: the early Fayum Neolithic (5200 BC) with roots in the Near East and the second Moerian phase (3500 BC) with affinities to the Sahara, particularly cultures from Siwa. D. L. Holmes's detailed lithic studies also view Moerian tools as Saharan in character, but she points to Kharga Oasis as their possible source.

The delta site of Merimde, a contemporary of the Fayum, offers an even closer look into the Neolithic lifestyle. Merimde, discovered by Hermann Junker, was the focus of seven seasons of excavation from 1929 to 1939, which were resumed in the late 1970s and early 1980s by J. Eiwanger and the German Institute of Archaeology. Merimde was originally founded on a pebbled terrace spur, the product of an ancient active wadi. The earliest (deepest) archaeological unit, Level I, was situated directly on the terrace. Excavators identified postholes surrounding fairly shallow round to oval pits, 2 or 3 meters in diameter. In some cases the oval pits contained areas of darkened soil that was thought to be evidence for fire hearths. Although there are differences between Merimde's Level I and subsequent levels (i.e., Levels II–V) in material

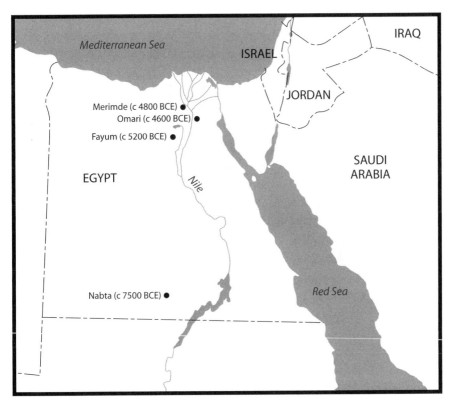

FIGURE 3.2. The easterly path of domestication as defined by the earliest known C-14 date for the respective site (by Ault and Flores).

remains, the resulting assemblages appear to demonstrate that the Neolithic culture appears in place from the beginning of Merimde's history. Like the early Fayum, Merimde's Level I seems to have its closest affinity with southwest Asia. Its ceramics with the incised herringbone pattern, lithics with their special type of blade edge retouching and polishing, and domestic species (wheat, barley, sheep, goat, and pig) as well as clay figurines all attest to eastern connections. The material remains of the upper levels do not modify this view of Merimde but tend to show it as a more evolved domestic economy.

The discovery of storage pits located near individual house units suggests that, unlike the Sahara and Fayum, each household was storing its own grain. The mat-lined depressions near some house pits could in fact be early examples of a threshing floor. Historically Egyptian grain was threshed in large depressions lined with hard earth and woven mats. However, Junker's poor control over the various aspects of the excavation makes these observations only suggestive rather than conclusive. What can be stated is that no clusters of storage pits were uncovered.

Merimde lithics offer a number of additional insights into the evolving culture. The raw materials used to fashion stone tools change between Levels I and II. Two factors may be responsible for this shift; first, by Level II times, the pebbles so often used in Level I lithics lie under a layer of sediments, making them more difficult to recover. Also, advances in lithic technology such as pressure flaking, bifacial retouch, and polishing required more homogenous types of stone, not readily available from the local wadi terrace but could be found in nearby geologic formations.

Eiwanger believes Level II had more of an African influence than eastern, pointing out that both the harpoon and hard stone axes have their closest affinity to the First Cataract region. Merimde Levels III–V take on a village-like appearance, with housing arranged along paths or streets and an increasing richness of material culture.

The site of Omari differs from Merimde in a number of ways: It is located on the east bank of the Nile, which offers a direct connection to southwest Asia via Sinai and to both Upper Egypt and the Delta. Also, Omari was really composed of two settlements (Omari A and C) and a cemetery (Omari B). Omari pottery is not like that of Merimde or the Fayum, but resembles more closely Palestinian Neolithic A and B ceramics. On the other hand, Omari lithics, in a general sense, follow the pattern of Merimde and Fayum with earlier tools made from flakes and blades gradually evolving into a bifacial tool kit.

The diversity of Omari food plants suggests to some scholars that the inhabitants had not reached a level of intensive agriculture where efforts are placed on a few or a single species, but such statements can only be taken as purely speculative. Not enough evidence has been gathered to confirm any issues concerning Omari agriculture.

Omari C, the Gebel Hof site, was situated on a 100-meter terrace overlooking Omari A and B. There, Egyptian archaeologists uncovered a reed enclosure within which they found a large jar and an oval pit containing carbonized cereals. The archeological material is similar to Omari A and B and thus it is thought to be their contemporary. Perhaps, a lookout point or a shelter from annual floods, which seem to have reached the Omari A settlement as evidenced by thin layers of precipitated salts in the stratigraphy.

Remains of the earliest known domestic donkey from Egypt was recovered from Omari – as were Red Sea shells, galena, and grey flint – suggesting connections with Sinai and further east, with the donkey, the main beast of burden for thousands of years, being the likely cargo carrier.

In general Omari's settlements are not as complex as Merimde, having neither polished black pottery, artistic products, or architecture. Rather, Omari may represent a typical Egyptian community of its day, imbedded in and taking advantage of its local micro-environment. Radiocarbon dates suggest a 200-year occupation (4600–4400 BC) corresponding to the more recent levels of Merimde.

EGYPT'S AGRICULTURAL ORIGINS

Summarizing the current evidence, we can posit a model for the introduction and spread of a domestic-based economy in Egypt. The general trend of a Neolithic-type lifestyle flowing from the Western Desert to the Fayum and into the Western Delta and Nile Valley may reflect the introductory path of domestic forms and their adoption into the Egyptian economy: from mobile hunter gatherer to mobile pastoralist to the more sedentary Nile dweller.

The adoption of domesticates into the desert/savanna lifestyle was simply an addition of resources, offering more stability to the established mobile lifestyle. In areas where resource productivity was more stable, such as the Fayum and Nile, increased sedentism was already part of the lifestyle, and the addition of domestic species simply added to that already established tendency. Eventually it became more beneficial to maintain a permanent residency to help with crops and the collection of other locally abundant wild resources. As arid conditions continued to prevail, populations shifted to more permanent sources of water, increasing the population density and the need for food, thereby creating greater reliability on domestic forms.

This begs the question of where we might seek more specific types of evidence to support or refute our model for Egypt's transition to the Neolithic. Like any good investigator, the archaeologist needs to establish what clues might be important in the search and where the best place might be to look. Because the Nile was at an extremely low level at this time, any riverside campsites and dwellings are now covered by meters of sediments from subsequent annual floods, leaving us to seek evidence elsewhere.

One obvious point of reference would be a review of available information in other regions, such as southwest Asia, where scholars have found information similar to what we seek. As we do so, two areas of interest emerge from a literature search of early agriculture in southwest Asia and elsewhere: population density and the "intensity" of biological interaction.

For millions of years, human population densities were low and groups were highly mobile. The impact of human activity on a given species was thus negligible in that humans were not in one place long enough and in sufficient numbers to create long-term effects on their targeted species. Then from 15,000 to 8000 years ago, major climatic changes forced many people to shift away from traditional big game hunting practices to focus on more intense hunting/harvesting of smaller species of mammals, fish, shellfish, birds, and plants. Evidence for this shift can be seen in the concurrent shift in tools: recall Egypt's late Paleolithic shift to microlithic tools, the discovery of smaller, well-made projectile points (arrow and dart), and the use of mortars and pestles for grinding plant seeds. By 8000 BC everyone was still practicing hunting and gathering, but in a much more diversified way than in previous periods. Some folks still adhered to the long-established big-game hunting traditions, whereas others hunted small game or fished, and still others intensively collected plants.

In many, if not most cultures, people practiced a combination of these pursuits, perhaps emphasizing one or a couple of resources. The phenomenon of food storage also seems to be linked to a number of hunter-gatherer groups pursuing these new resources. Some groups stored large amounts of food; others did not, but those groups that did store large quantities had several things in common:

* seasonally abundant food resources,
* high human-population densities,
* greater degree of sedentism, and
* evidence of a social hierarchy.

A reaction to an abundant food resource, even a seasonally available one, is an increase in population density: Because the area is able to support more people, they congregate there. In some parts of the world such as southwest Asia, the coexistence between food species and humans was a contributor to genetic changes that led to co-dependency. With the human population increasing, resulting in more intensive collecting, harvesting or hunting, the prey species, over time, adapted to this new challenge. Some of these changes served humans as well as the targeted plant or animal, initiating the first stages of a domestication process. It should be understood that humans involved in the initial stages of domestication did not set out intentionally to create species with certain characteristics but rather did so unintentionally by merely culling, collecting, or otherwise intensely engaging with wild forms.

Egypt, however, followed a slightly different path than southwest Asia in that it appears nonindigenous, domesticated species were adopted into existing traditions. How we might acquire a better understanding of this process has become an obsession with some archaeologists.

ARCHAEOLOGY AND SAMPLING

The desert regions west of the Nile offer some of the most intriguing evidence related to early Neolithic lifestyles: Recent research has shown that sites there are of the appropriate age and, because they have not been affected by seasonal flooding, are generally accessible. But where should we seek the archaeological data to answer our questions? Sampling is the obvious first step in the process.

Sampling of one type or another permeates all aspects of archaeology: It is simply the means by which archaeologists make inferences about a large population of artifacts from a precisely collected sample. Sampling – the selection of a small part or quantity intended to yield knowledge of the whole – has been in use since the beginnings of archaeology. In fact, one could say archaeology *is* sampling, in the sense that all archaeologists attempt to make generalizations, at least on some level, from limited data. Archaeologists have neither the time nor the resources to excavate every site and artifact ever made, nor would it be particularly wise to do so given that theories and methods are still evolving. And even if archaeologists did have the entire archaeological record to work with, it would still only represent a portion of ancient human behavior patterns. Materials that do not preserve well will always be underrepresented in archaeological contexts, and, of course, there are many human behaviors that leave no material trace at all. Yet it is by recognizing and understanding the limitations of the data with which archaeologists have to work that meaningful conclusions can be drawn.

For much of its history, sampling in archaeology was intuitive and non-probabilistic. Discussions regarding the "representativeness" of a sample, such as surface sherd collections, began in the early twentieth century (e.g., Kroeber 1916 and Spier 1917), but the lack of developed statistical theory necessarily hindered such efforts. Advances in statistical theory made in the 1930s began to trickle into archaeology during the 1940s and 1950s, but it was not until the 1960s with Binford's explicit advocacy of probabilistic sampling methods for regional surveys that more formal sampling methods took hold. With the "scientific" goals of processual archaeology and advances in computing technology in the 1970s and 1980s, the application of formal statistical sampling strategies became widespread. Today, sampling is used in every aspect of archaeology, from locating sites by surveying, to selecting areas of a site to excavate, to constructing chronological frameworks from artifact typologies, to collecting tiny portions of artifacts for use in chemical analysis.

Archaeologists use many kinds of sampling methods, and often even combine them. In general, they can be divided into two types: probability sampling and non-probability sampling. All probability sampling methods utilize some form of random selection in order to eliminate bias. In employing random selection, the researcher ensures that different units in the population have equal probabilities of being chosen. Common probability sampling strategies used by archaeologists include simple random sampling, systematic sampling, stratified sampling, and cluster sampling. These methods can stand alone or be combined (multistage sampling) depending on the research problem. Orton (2000) provides a comprehensive discussion of these methods and their application to archaeology at all levels. What is vital is that these various ways of probability sampling allow us to extrapolate from the sample to the larger whole, *and* their likely margins of error – the probability that the sample accurately represents the whole – can be calculated using statistical procedures.

Non-probability sampling is any sampling method where the selection of units is not random, either because it is based on prior information and/or assumptions (purposive sampling) or because of circumstantial constraints (accidental or convenience sampling). For instance, the selection of sites to excavate based on surface remains is a type of purposive sampling. One is likely to locate sites in this manner, but one has no idea how many sites may have been overlooked because no surface features remain. Accidental or convenience sampling is just as the name implies; the discovery of an ancient site during modern construction is but one example. Because non-probability sampling does not allow one to gauge the representativeness of the sample, it lacks the potential for generalization. On the whole, non-probability sampling is useful for situations where one needs to reach a targeted sample quickly and where sampling for proportionality is not the primary concern; probability sampling is more useful when one does not have a priori knowledge of the target population and when one wishes to draw general conclusions.

The most important characteristic of any sample collected for the purpose of making inferences about a larger population is how well it represents that population. Common strategies for collecting a sample include random, stratified, and systematic. For example, if one had twelve sites and only time and money to do five, one could give each site a number and randomly choose five from a hat. As long as each site has an equal chance of being picked, random sampling has been achieved. Pure random sampling is often done when the researcher knows little about the area or the study area is extremely uniform, such as a swath of flat desert with a host of seemingly similar artifact scatters. If, however, six of twelve sites were along the Nile and six were in the desert margins, one might stratify the sample, thereby randomly choosing an equal number of sites from each environmental zone (the Nile and desert). Stratified sampling is used when some information important to answering the posed questions is incorporated into the recovery strategy. If one were interested in near-shore versus offshore activities, sampling from both environments would be important and thus a stratified sampling design would be a good course of action.

In some instances there might be systematically placed features or evidence for a number of different types of structures that one wants to include in excavations. A simple random sample might create clusters and miss the systematically placed features, or might not provide a sample of each type of structure. In such cases, a systematic random sample might be taken whereby collection units are spaced at equal intervals throughout the sampling area, with only the sampling interval being selected randomly. For example, after a site is divided into 5 × 5 meter sampling units, a sampling interval, called a sampling fraction, is chosen (a decision often based on time and money); the first unit is picked randomly and thereafter each unit is designated by the sampling interval. If funds and time allow for one-fifth of a site to be excavated, the sampling fraction is one in five and a random number (between one and five) is drawn to identify the first unit, let us say four; thereafter the eighth, twelfth, sixteenth . . . units are selected. The system has the obvious benefit of distributing the sample more evenly across the site.

Cluster sampling is used when previous knowledge of the target population shows that natural groupings or "clusters" are present. For example, in a given region previous research has shown that there are habitation sites, cemeteries, herding sites, and fishing camps. To take advantage of this knowledge, like sites are clustered and within each of these groupings, sites are chosen for study. Use of this method ensures that a sample from each site type is included in the study, something that a more randomized strategy could miss.

How one knows which sampling design to employ for a given situation is a matter of playing the odds. Choosing the appropriate technique is a combination of the archaeologist's experience of "reading the site and its potential" coupled with an understanding of sampling designs. How well the chosen technique fits the situation can only be evaluated once the data has been collected, analyzed, and measured against the original problem. Archaeologists are not always correct in their choices of design and as I can attest, "randomness" is a fickle ally; more than once an important find was missed by mere centimeters because it fell just outside of a randomly chosen unit.

As a basic rule of thumb, when nothing is known about an area, and that area is homogenous, a simple random or systematic random sample is employed.

If definable areas are present, be they known archaeological features or natural ones, a stratified or clustered sample might offer a better chance of collecting a representative sample of artifacts.

Assessing how representative a sample might be is as much art as science. The goal of parametric sampling is to obtain an accurate reflection of the population, whether that population is the different types of sites in a region or the features and artifacts of an ancient village. The sample then offers a reliable means to make inferences about the entire population without having to actually tally each individual member of that population.

In general, a 10 percent sample of the population is sought, but this number is really more an accepted standard than a guarantee of success. One way to assess an archaeological sample is through redundancy. For example, when collecting stone tools or pieces of pottery, the first object one picks up will be unique, the second object picked up may likewise be unique, but as one continues to collect, one will start to encounter objects like those already collected. Over time, the frequency at which one finds new types of stone tools or pottery becomes rare; one's additions simply add to the frequency of already collected types. When artifact classes have stabilized into an ordinal arrangement, redundancy has likely been achieved; that is, continued sampling serves only to add to the number of artifacts in an already established sequence of abundance (Type A remains most abundant, Type B is next, followed by Type C, etc.) (Figure 3.3).

Unfortunately, the only way to know for sure if the sample is truly representative is to collect the entire site. Archaeologists do, however, recognize the fact that their samples may be less than representative and may even violate some of the basic laws of statistical inference, but we push forward, knowing that our discipline is not one of absolutes and that every piece of evidence is important. Fortunately, there are statistical means to assess the sample and as more sites of the same type are collected and similar results are produced, the likelihood of "representativeness" increases exponentially.

SAMPLING IN PRACTICE

Perhaps nowhere is the Neolithic transition more apparent than in the Fayum depression, and work in the area provides a good exercise in sampling design. Not only was there a vibrant Epipaleolithic tradition living along the shore of the lake, but some of the earliest sites dated to the Neolithic are located here as well. But even here, the "why" and "how" of the Neolithic transition remains difficult to decipher.

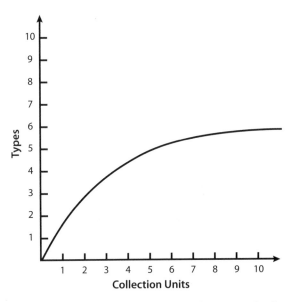

FIGURE 3.3. The graph represents sampling to a redundancy: as the curve levels, continued sampling adds only types already collected (by Ault and Flores).

Today the Fayum and its lake, Birket Qarun, lie about 44 meters below sea level. The lake is extremely saline and essentially void of any indigenous animal life. During the Epipaleolithic, however, the lake was connected to the Nile by a natural channel that replenished its waters every year during the annual flood. The area was home to a variety of fish, waterfowl, and wild animals. Along the lake's shores and in the surrounding marshes, groups of people belonging to the Epipaleolithic Qarunian or Fayum B culture thrived. Qarunian sites, dating from about 6240 to 5480 BC, can be found all along the old lake shoreline (Figure 3.4). These sites appear to be campsites, often with remains of fish and animals strewn about the hearths. Qarunian tools were small-backed blades and bladelettes of the microlithic tradition. With the onset of lower-level Nile floods beginning about 5480 BC, the lake's water was no longer replenished, the flood height having fallen below the elevation of the channel feeding the lake. When the lake disappeared, the Qarunian culture disappeared as well: Archaeologists have found little evidence of any occupation of the Fayum basin for nearly 300 years, after which a fully Neolithic people occupied the shorelines of the revitalized lake.

Intrigued by Caton-Thompson's finds, I visited the Fayum with a group of senior scholars, and along the ancient shoreline, we noted scatters of artifacts extending many kilometers into the desert. The scatters were sometimes quite dense and close to one another, but at other times separated by

FIGURE 3.4. Ancient Fayum lake shoreline where Epi-paleolitc tools have been recovered (photo by D. J. Brewer).

considerable distance. Artifacts included backed bladelettes of the Epipaleolithic period, concave points, and Predynastic and Old Kingdom pottery. Because our interest was the Neolithic transition, we focused on the Epipaleolithic and Neolithic evidence, but these artifacts could be found all along the ancient lake shore, suggesting to us that Caton-Thompson's village-like Kom K and W were actually unique, and thus they alone would not give us a full accounting of ancient Fayum life. Clearly what was needed was a regional sampling approach.

Regional archaeology is simply moving focus from the site to the region, in our case from Kom W and K to the larger Fayum lake area. The rationale is that the ancient inhabitants of Kom W and K were not limited to these archaeological sites but utilized resources across the entire region. The site was simply an important component in their wider use of the landscape – the many sites located along the lake offer perfect evidence of this fact. How far beyond the Fayum the ancient inhabitants traveled we might never know, but certainly the lake environment was an important part of their livelihood.

The first step in creating our design was to define the region (Figure 3.5a). This was accomplished using topographic maps, aerial photos (satellite photos not being available at the time), and simple on-ground surveys. Based on the

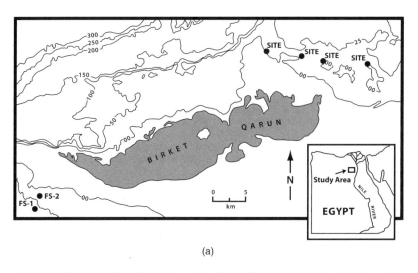

(a)

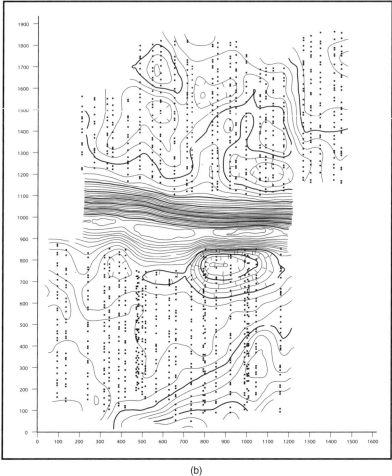

(b)

FIGURE 3.5. The Fayum region as defined by the Fayum Archaeological Project showing sites (a), transects and collection units (b) (Ault and Flores after Brewer 1989, figure 31 and Wenke et al. 1988, figure 4).

maps, we defined the ancient drainage basin and its shorelines. Walking perpendicular to the ancient shoreline and into the desert, we noted when artifact concentrations declined to the point of being rare to virtually nonexistent. We defined this as our regional boundary and then developed a site-sampling strategy.

Site surveys are essentially a means to locate a representative sample of sites within the larger region. As in any sampling design, achieving a representative sample is the goal. In this case we wanted to recover information on the different site types in the area. Once these had been defined, collection/excavation strategies could be developed to recover samples from the different site types.

Survey methods range from simply walking an area, as we did, in trying to determine the limits of the region to systematic surveys where on-ground units are defined and inspected. The units usually employed are transects or quadrants. A quadrant design resembles a chessboard. The area to be surveyed is divided into equal-sized quadrants, and they are selected randomly for inspection. A transect design would be a complete row running from one side of the chessboard to the other. A chessboard would then have eight possible transects, from which a sample could be randomly chosen for survey. All the rules of sampling and associated problems with different designs discussed previously apply to the selection of units to be surveyed.

Because our interests were as much in gaining some knowledge about the different types of sites in the region as to where they might be located, a transect survey was chosen. Based on our knowledge of Kom K and W and our initial foot survey to define the limits of the region, we felt that artifact densities as well as types of artifacts changed based on their distance from the lake. Our best chance to note these differences would be to divide the area into transects using the current lake as the starting point. The region was thus divided into five-meter–wide transects emanating from the lake and extending out into the desert, like spokes from the hub of a wagon wheel. Transects were chosen in a systematic random design in order to best cover the area.

As is often the case in archaeology, the plans established in the comforts of the office need revision when implemented in the field. Our transects, as we found out, were perfectly designed for their purpose: locating artifact scatters relative to the lake. Along the northern shore everything moved perfectly and as expected, offering a number of sites that could be sampled for later study. What we did not count on was the enormity of the scatters on the southwestern part of the lake, which in essence amounted to one huge artifact scatter stretching for kilometers: Defining sites within this area seemed an arbitrary decision. It was not too difficult to surmise that this area was important and worthy of intensive study, so we quickly designed a nested sampling scheme. Within this large concentration of continuous artifacts we first divided the area into transects and randomly chose 48 for collections. These lines were then divided into 5 × 5 meter collection units, of which 1257 were randomly selected for study Figure 3.5b.

On the north side of the lake four sites were chosen for study, two Paleolithic and two Neolithic occupations. Because the sites were discrete scatters with definable boundaries, they were gridded into 5 × 5-meter units for collection with all faunal remains and artifacts collected. Test excavations were also done, but in each case the artifacts seemed to be limited to the surface.

One of the most interesting aspects of the study was the faunal remains. Both Neolithic and Epipaleolithic Fayum cultures hunted and fished for the same species with similar preferences and at the same time of year. "Seasonality," the timing each year a task is carried out, was gained through a specialized study of the growth rings of catfish, a measurement similar to that of tree rings. The only apparent difference between the faunal assemblages was that the Neolithic peoples added some domestic species, mostly sheep and goat, to their diet. The large number of bones from fish and other wild animals suggest that at least part of the Neolithic Fayum population maintained a mobile lifestyle, much like their Epipaleolithic predecessors.

The Fayum thus fits nicely into our developing model of increasing sedentism and greater dependence on a domestic-based economy as one moves from the Western Desert east to the Nile Valley, through time.

4

A CULTURAL TRANSFORMATION: EXPLAINING OR DESCRIBING THE PAST

One of the most impressive accomplishments of the ancient Egyptians was their rapid cultural transformation in the fifth and fourth millennia BC from a society based on simple agricultural villages to the creation of a complex and organized, socially stratified society. What were the dynamics that caused people and cultures to change as they did? What forces propelled Egypt from simple farming to "high civilization"? Why was Egypt fundamentally similar in its developmental trajectory and characteristics to other ancient civilizations, and why and how did it differ, are all questions archaeologists have posed and attempted to answer for decades.

Around 4500 BC, the Nile Valley and Delta appear to have been occupied by people living in small, functionally similar agricultural communities that were only weakly interconnected politically and economically. By around 3050 BC, Egypt had aligned itself under a single ruler, and over the next 500 years continued to coalesce into an integrated, hierarchically stratified society whose ruler expressed power through a massive bureaucracy that touched virtually every person along the Nile and, through economic and military force, extended that reach throughout the Mediterranean region.

CULTURE IN TRANSITION

Because written records did not appear until very late in the sociopolitical process, the study of Egypt's formative period relies almost exclusively on the archaeological interpretation of stoneware, faunal and floral remains, habitation sites, cemeteries, and pottery – artifacts that are excellent for snapshots of the past but much less accurate when used to define long-term sociopolitical trends. Thus our archaeological finds are akin to understanding the plot of a complicated motion picture from the study of a few damaged still photographs. Furthermore, at least until recently, the archaeological record played only a limited role in explanations of Egypt's early social complexity.

Although a tremendously rich trove of information has been collected by Egyptologists working in the historical paradigm, the type of data needed to answer processual archaeological questions (such as ancient demography, economies, and settlement patterns) requires a different approach. The data that has been traditionally retrieved about Egypt has been in the form of straightforward efforts to reconstruct some aspect of ancient Egyptian society or to establish casual links between ecological, technological, and demographic variables on the one hand, and sociopolitical variables on the other. Questions involving sociopolitical processes require data collected in such a manner that they can be contrasted across time, space, and cultures.

Obviously, the theoretical paradigm employed dictates what analytical units are created. There are, however, no powerful theories of archaeology that tell us how ancient complex societies should best be studied, categorized, or measured for the purpose of explaining their origin. The very definition of "complex society" is a paradox: as elsewhere, it is defined here in a traditional sense involving a nonquantitative composite of monumental architecture, inferred mortuary cults, rank and wealth hierarchies, and specialized craft production – essentially a trait list compiled from data collected through a historical line of inquiry. The definition at best is descriptive, but certainly not analytical or processual.

Beyond the seemingly contradictory use of historic-based definitions in so-called scientific archaeology, post-processual archaeologists would label these very lines of inquiry as techno-environmental determinism, functional argumentation, or cultural ecological possibilism, and believe that such research is an extremely limited form of analysis, epistemologically sterile and morally wrong in its ethnocentrism and imperialism.

So how are we as archaeologists to proceed? Clearly we must begin by understanding the types of problems and related data collection strategies that those working in the historical paradigm have employed and how these discoveries have shaped our way of thinking about Egypt. For example, early attempts to understand how Egypt evolved from an egalitarian, village-based economy to the political sophistication of the First Dynasty were derived initially from historical texts and myth, and the focus was on the transformative figure Menes or his real-life counterpart. Interestingly, similar themes are known from other cultures: Figures such as Menes, Agamemnon, Romulus, and David (mythical or real) assembled armies, instituted laws and administration, and imposed taxation, all in a relatively few years. Could these accounts be factually correct in all circumstances? At least in Egypt, with the development of region-wide archaeological chronologies and the refinement of dating techniques, it is clear that the rise to state-level complexity was a process taking many centuries, not the work of a single individual.

Nevertheless, to the frustration of many, even though Egypt's rise to state-level complexity can now be defined in terms of centuries rather than millennia and our comprehension of regional events, changing demographics, and economies (as well as details of administrative leadership) have increased significantly, the precise steps by which Egypt coalesced into the first great territorial state remain elusive. Perhaps complicating the matter is the fact that archaeological conceptions of state formation have changed markedly in the course of the past century. Archaeologists and historians studying Egypt now define the state more complexly (e.g., social stratification, the presence of cities, kingship, hierarchical political control, etc.), and by doing so have in effect raised the bar of difficulty in answering the "origins" question, perhaps to unattainable levels. To date, there remains no way to prove that any one of these more recently defined lines of research, whether it be historical, processual or post-processual, is better than another.

Interestingly, sociologists grapple with some of the same problems as do archaeologists even though the sociologist is viewing the actual phenomenon as it occurs or has access to a plethora of eyewitness accounts of a recent historical event. This would suggest that archaeologists may be interested in solving sociological questions that our data simply are not equipped to answer. Clearly archaeology needs to review its goals and seek answers to answerable questions.

Regardless of the possibility of finding a single, coherent explanation to the origin of Egypt or any other state-level society, archaeologists of many different theoretical inclinations seem to be searching for a way to deal with what they presume to be the determining effects of intrinsically social, political, and ideological forces that led to social complexity. The research results do show that some lines of inquiry better account for historical events in one instance than another.

POTTERY AND EGYPT'S FORMATIVE PERIOD

Egypt's formative or Predynastic Period was first introduced to the archaeological community in 1896 when Jacques de Morgan, excavating the cemeteries of Abydos, recovered bone and ivory jewelry, figurines, slate palettes, beautiful flaked flint tools, and most important, pottery of a style different than that of the later Dynastic Period (Figure 4.1a, b). He asserted that these graves and

(a)

(b)

FIGURE 4.1. (a) and (b) Examples of classic Naqada Period artifacts (Copyright Carnegie Museum of Natural History).

those from other nearby sites predated Dynasty 1 – a profound declaration given he had no stratigraphic or other corroborating evidence.

Pottery, probably more so than any other artifact class, has defined the Predynastic Period – both de Morgan's original proclamation and Petrie's affirmation relied heavily on pottery. As pottery was used by virtually all Predynastic peoples because it is durable, numerically abundant, and most important, because it changes stylistically, it has served as a tool to denote the passage of time, identify functional areas and like the stone tools of the Paleolithic, Predynastic pottery offers potential clues to cultural affiliation, technological skill, and cross-cultural contacts, to name just a few of its archaeological uses.

Most archaeological studies of pottery are of three types: classification, decorative analysis, and compositional. Compositional studies are usually technical investigations that focus on the ingredients of the ceramic clay and the properties conferred by those ingredients. Study of the decorative motifs, whether painted, incised, or molded on the vessel, offers insights into the creators' aesthetic perceptions and ideological systems. Classification studies compare groups of ceramics indicative of a particular culture at a given time in order to create chronologies, identify site function, or shed light on broader issues of cultural expansion, trade, communication, and complexity.

Archaeologists classify pots in a number of different ways. Regardless of method, the vessel (or fragment) is at some point placed in a group or, in formal terms, a "class" based on certain observable criteria. The classification of pots, like that of plants or animals, is based on the principle that the similarity of entities within a group does not occur by chance but reflects significant relationships. In the case of pottery, classification is usually based on certain common features of material, construction technique, and vessel form such that when the class is properly defined, an archaeologist can recognize other examples when they occur.

Once defined, a class of objects is often referred to as a type. This is a term borrowed from biology where the first published example of a species becomes the "type specimen" and those collected with it become the type series. These archaeological types are then used to corroborate later finds.

There has been much debate as to whether archaeological types are "real" in the sense that they portray some image that the ancient potter was trying to emulate, or whether types are simply a creation of the analyst. Regardless, when properly created and directed to the appropriate question, types serve as important archaeological tools. For example, Petrie's wavy handle jars – a type – clearly reflected different Predynastic periods (see Figure 2.2).

In Egypt, ceramic analysis has evolved into a specialized field within archaeology, with standardized terms relating to its description, identification, and study. Egyptian archaeologists most often employ the taxonomic approach to pottery classification, which focuses on a combination of vessel characteristics or attributes. The choice of attributes depends on the problem the archaeologist wishes to investigate. Chronological questions such as those addressed by Petrie's work are the most common and employ combinations of stylistic and functional attributes that change through time.

There has been, however, little discussion on the difference between stylistic and functional attributes in Egyptian ceramic analysis. The distinction between the two is important because they behave differently over time. Referring back to our biological analogy of type, ceramic traits that have real-life value such as water-impermeable clay, inclusions to increase strength, or a specific shape fitted to a specific purpose, such as holding or carrying water, are functionally based traits. They exist because they proved to be better than traits or techniques employed previously. Traits that are purely neutral, that can change without affecting the use of the vessel, such as decorative patterns, are stylistic. A stylistic trait can come into and go out of fashion without affecting the function of the pot, but a functional trait is replaced "ideally" when a new attribute has proven to be better. Changes in inclusions, clay mixtures, shapes, thicknesses, or building techniques might all be examples of improvements in functionality of a vessel. Clearly, we need to be wary of the two trait types when including them in a classification system.

The process of classification should not be confused with identification, which refers to assigning objects to established classes previously defined. By employing Petrie's sequence dating system (Figure 4.2), we are in effect identifying vessels and placing them within an established sequence. Analyzing a new, previously unclassified set of pottery vessels and placing them within newly defined groups is classification, which constitutes a much more daunting task than simple identification.

Pottery types can be formed through a hierarchal or paradigmatic use of attributes. In a paradigmatic approach, each ceramic attribute is weighed equally whereas the hierarchical approach gives preference to certain attributes, much like the biological taxonomic system. Each approach has its supporters and detractors. Proponents of paradigmatic classification believe that applying a hierarchical system is artificially ascribing importance to an attribute. They also believe that if all attributes are treated equally, one is allowed to discover which attributes are important. For example, when the hierarchical system most commonly used in Egypt today is employed, the type

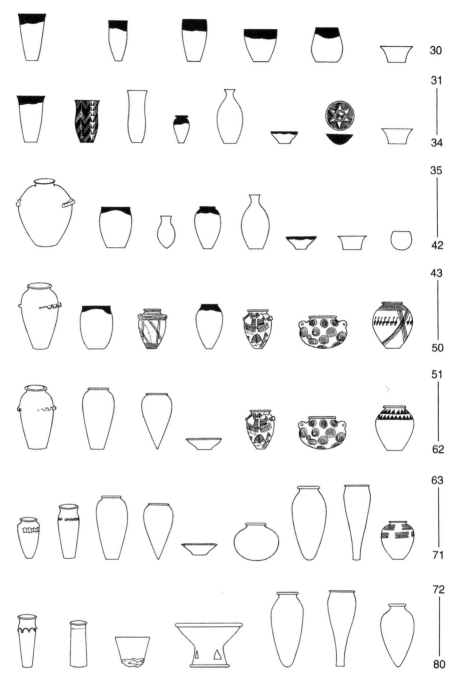

FIGURE 4.2. Petrie's ceramic sequence dating system and the associated "sequence date." He purposely left space at the beginning and end of his chronology (0–30 and 80–100) for future discoveries (after Brewer and Teeter 2007, figure 1.2).

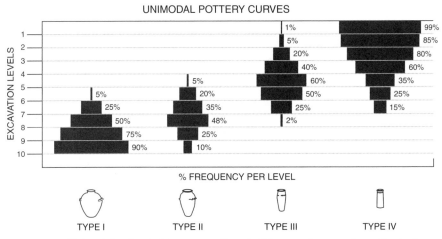

FIGURE 4.3. Unimodal or battleship curves reflect the lifespan of a type where after its intro-duction it increases in popularity and then declines as it is replaced by another type (by Jackie Gardner).

of clay is often one of the first dividing criteria. Wavy handle jars would thus first be separated from other vessels because they were made of marl clay. From this point they would be further divided into less inclusive groups. The issue here is: How would a vessel that resembles a wavy handle jar in every respect except clay be classified? In the hierarchal system, it could be a new type; however, in a paradigmatic classification, this would not necessarily be the case. In the end, whatever system is applied needs to address the archaeological questions posed.

The use of pottery types in chronology building has two major applications, cross dating and sequence dating. In cross dating, a particular ceramic well known at one site or region is "identified" at another site, showing that the two sites are contemporaneous. Sequence dating, better known today as seriation, orders items in a series. One means of ordering ceramics is through their similarity in appearance (à la Petrie). Seriation becomes a dating method when the sequence is correlated with the passage of time. This is carried out based on the assumption that the vessel type will increase and then decrease in popularity through time. By drawing a simple analogy: A particular toy, movie, or video game after a successful introduction to the marketplace will often grow in popularity, then over time reach a peak, and finally lose its popularity as other movies or games come on the market. This is often portrayed in terms of a unimodal or "battleship" curve (Figure 4.3). Like a movie or video game, pottery types follow similar patterns such that their introduction is followed by an increase in popularity (i.e., use), only to later fall out of use as other

TABLE 4.1. *Petrie's SD dates and the derivation of the Predynastic sequence*

Date (BC)	SD	Upper Egypt	Lower Egypt
3000		Dynasty 1 (Naqada IIIc)	Dynasty 1 (Naqada IIIc)
		Dynasty 0 (Naqada IIIb)	Dynasty 0 (Naqada IIIb)
	63–75		
3100		Protodynastic (Nagada IIIa)	Nagada IIIa
3300			
3400	40/45–63	Late Gerzean (Nagada IIc-d)	Late Gerzean (Ma'adian)
3500	38–40/45	Early Gerzean (Nagada IIb)	
3650		(Nagada IIa)	Omari B (?)
3750	30–38	Amratian (Nagada Ia-c)	Omari A (?)
4400		Badarian	
4800			Merimden
5200			Fayum A

forms increase in popularity. This is essentially the basis of the Predynastic system developed by Petrie (and later improved upon by modern scholars), the important factor being that certain points along the path can be anchored in time.

The dating system most widely used in Egypt today is the so-called Stufe System developed by the German archaeologist Werner Kaiser using pottery and associated artifacts. Kaiser, like other archaeologists, noted the usefulness of Petrie's sequence dating (SD) system but was aware of its shortcomings. For example, the SD dates were in no way indicative of a given number of passing years. A date of SD 75 could correspond to a time period three times longer than any other SD date. Petrie himself was aware of this, noting that SD 38–40 represented a different amount of time than SD 40–45.

Although sequence dating and the resulting ordering of classes was never designed to supply true chronological dates, Kaiser noted how ceramic vessels, and their associations with different types of artifacts, differed horizontally across sites. At Armont, for example, Kaiser observed that a cemetery containing some 170 graves shifted from south to north over time. By plotting the presence of specific pottery types across a map of the site, he was able to demonstrate that the pottery clustered in different patterns that represented different periods of time. For example, by utilizing Petrie's black-topped red ware, he was able to identify three major periods (Stufe I, II, and III) and could further subdivide these into eleven temporal phases. Kaiser then defined his stages in terms of Petrie's SD system, employing a dating chronology used by nearly all archaeologists working in Egypt today (Table 4.1).

Beyond chronology building, ceramics continue to offer important insights into Egypt's past. For example, archaeologists are often interested in knowing what function a site or part of a site once held, and ceramic analysis can help in such determinations.

The simplest means to determine vessel function is through analogy: Narrow-necked vessels are likely to be used for transporting liquids because less will spill from their opening than from wide-mouthed vessels; round bases are advantageous for cooking vessels because they transmit heat easily and are less susceptible to breakage from thermal stress than flat-based vessels, and so on.

Those assessing site function using pottery, usually adhere to the assumption that the ceramic remains were used in the area of recovery. This should not, however, be taken as a given but must be corroborated with associated archaeological finds. In one study, 150 meters separated fragments of a single pot. There are circumstances, however, where good work provides convincing evidence. The analysis of diverse ceramic assemblages for the large Predynastic town of Hierakonpolis offers just such an example.

By 3500 BC Hierakonpolis could be described as a small city with many neighborhoods, stretching some three kilometers along the Nile. In an area pockmarked by the activity of looters, archaeologists chose to excavate in a location particularly rich in ceramic sherds. There they made a most remarkable find: a well-preserved house and a craftsman's workshop.

Predynastic dwellings are rare and poorly preserved but this small rectangular semi-subterranean house could be reconstructed with accuracy, as could the associated workshop. It seems the owner was a potter and the workshop included a pottery oven that apparently caught fire, with fire spreading to the nearby house. The house was 4 × 3.5 meters, with a mudbrick foundation and a wood post frame for securing the reed mats that formed the walls and ceiling. The entire structure was covered with a mixture of mud, dung, and brick rubble.

The workshop was a 5 × 6–meter oval platform with numerous depressions carved into it. Each depression contained a large, straw-tempered pottery vessel (50–80 centimeters wide and nearly 1 meter tall) supported by long triangular ceramic logs. These large vessels served as firing chambers for smaller vessels. The pottery produced had a unique trademark – a crescent-shaped thumbprint applied just beneath the rim of the pot. Large round-bottom pots bearing the maker's mark were recovered all around the workshop and throughout the neighborhood.

The workshop was separated from the house by about 5 meters, but somehow the kiln fire spread to the home, which was destroyed with living accouterments intact. In fact, the charred wood logs used to frame the house were recovered exactly where they fell. In the house was a small brick-lined depression thought to be a hearth for cooking and heating in one corner, and an upturned pot in another corner. By the arrangement of the support poles, it appeared there was an open porch to the house, and around the house was a light reed fence probably used to hold animals.

Following the fire, the house was rebuilt (this time farther from the kiln). Because the identifying pottery trademark can be seen for many generations after the accident, we assume the potter not only survived the fire but trained subsequent generations in pottery making.

Through diligent analyses of over 350,000 sherds, archaeologists could quite convincingly identify the function of this particular area of the town. The fact that the assemblage was dominated by straw-tempered pottery (98 percent), which is never found in burial contexts, makes it quite reasonable to conclude that this area was a manufacturing center for utilitarian wares. Further pottery analysis at Hierakonpolis has also identified a brewery and a bakery, as well as other functional areas.

The Hierakonpolis study, along with other ceramic studies, has added to our understanding of how Egypt came to be. In her study of the pottery from Hememieh, Naqada, and Hierakonpolis, ceramicist Renee Friedman noted the diversity of styles from Amration settlements when compared to those recovered from cemeteries, the mortuary pottery being much more homogeneous. Significantly, she noted that this regional diversity in utilitarian pottery disappears by the mid-Gerzean period (Naqada IIc) and is replaced by a standardized, technologically superior, chaff-tempered, rough-ware pottery. This new pottery is identical in temper, manufacturing technique, and shape at all three sites and appears in conjunction with a suit of other specialized activities: a phenomenon also seen in the Delta, where local traditions initially dominate assemblages but later, Upper Egyptian pottery dominates.

Feinman, Kwaleski, and Blanton have equated this shift in ceramic production with growing administrative control of economic institutions. They note that meeting increased demands results in increased standardization of products as pottery workshops adopt new time-saving techniques such as the wheel or molds, and pottery making becomes more routinized. Also, there tends to be a decrease in the amount of time invested per vessel on nonfunctional (i.e., decoration) features. What this suggests is that by mid-Naqada II, economically, Egypt is beginning to coalesce into a larger, more

FIGURE 4.4. The hallmark "rippled pottery" of the Badarian culture. The ripple effect is made by dragging a serrated catfish spine or comb across the unfired clay vessel, then smoothing the marks with well-watered hands and firing the pot (UC 9011: Copyright of the Petrie Museum of Egyptian Archaeology, UCL).

centrally controlled society, creating a more efficient environment where ceramics are mass-produced and distributed over larger areas. At the very least it shows Egypt was becoming more economically centralized, and by inference, one might argue that economic centrality reflects a move to sociopolitical centrality.

POTTERY AND CULTURE

The earliest Predynastic valley culture was the Badarian, and the most distinctive product of Badarian culture was the pottery. Much if not all of our knowledge pertaining to Badarian ceramics comes from Brunton's classification, which was based predominantly on mortuary finds. In all, Brunton identified some sixty-two shapes ranging from shallow to deep and further subdivided them on the basis of the vessel base: flat, round, with or without carination. The unfired clay paste or "fabric" was mostly fine-grained Nile silt, mixed with straw, and fired to a brown color, but red and black vessels also occasionally occurred. The vessels were hand formed, often black-topped, and frequently rippled (Figure 4.4). Some of the finer rippled pots were burnished with a smooth stone. Brunton thought the rippling was a by-product of thinning the vessel walls, but one type of extremely thin and well-made vessel lacks the characteristic ripple effect. Another distinctive feature of the pottery vessels was the nearly straight lip; few pots possessed a neck or outwardly flared rim. There was also a large, simply made type of pottery, often soot blackened, suggesting it was used in cooking fires.

The recovery from burials of countless shell and stone bead necklaces, carved combs, cosmetic palettes, and jars filled with pigment strongly suggests that Badarian people exhibited a tendency toward ornamentation and display. Badarian graves also produced well-made ivory spoons, humanoid figurines of clay or ivory, animal amulets, and carved throwing sticks used to propel hunting darts (see Figure 4.5). Beautifully made hollow-based projectile points, remarkably similar to those of the Fayum, suggest contact between these areas. A few graves contained small copper tools and ornamental pins.

There is no sharp or distinct cultural break between the Badarians and the next identifiable valley culture, the Naqadans. Naqada I sites contain Badarian elements, and some late Badarian sites contain Naqada I elements. This would suggest an indigenous development for the culture, but it is not known whether Badarian evolved into Naqada I or whether both cultures had independent sources that later merged (Figure 4.6).

Like the Badarians, Naqada I dead were buried on their left side, in a contracted position, with the head to the south and facing westward. But it is at this time that we begin to see a small proportion of bodies being buried in large, well-equipped graves rather than simple pits. Wrapping the body in animal skins was less common, and wooden and clay coffins made their first appearance, although still rare. As in the Badarian, men, women, and children were buried throughout the cemetery without any sense of zoning.

The Badarian combed (rippled) pottery treatment still existed but soon faded out of style, whereas red-polished pottery became increasingly more common (Figure 4.7a, b). Black-topped redware pottery, a Predynastic hallmark, made its debut at this time; the blackened rim was an intentional modification of the typical redware vessel. Black-topped redware pottery was made from well-mixed and water-sorted (levigated) Nile silt, although late in the period some black-topped vessels were made from unlevigated silts and tempered with straw. The black top was thought to be created by subjecting the rim to smoke, but other plausible explanations have been given. The diversity of vessel shapes increased at this time, probably reflecting a wider use of ceramic vessels for different purposes. Black-topped bowls with everted rims, jars with concave and curving profiles, bottle-shaped vessels, hole-mouthed jars with a convex upper body, and pointed based jars are all new shapes.

Another feature of the pottery dated to this period is that many vessels were incised with signs known as pot-marks, usually made after firing (Figure 4.8a, b). The fact that the same signs were repeated on different pots

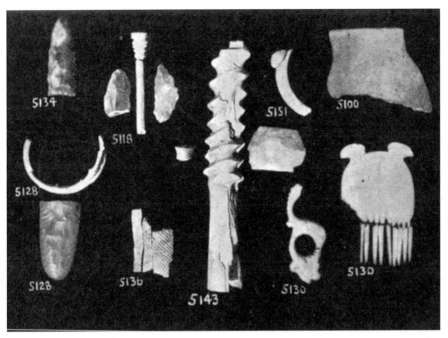

(a)

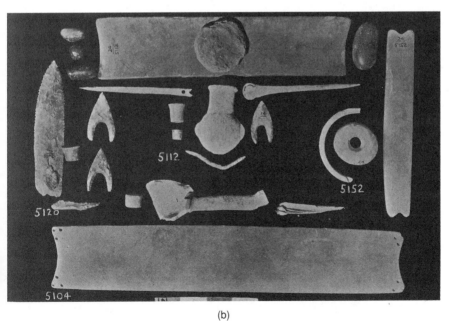

(b)

FIGURE 4.5. Typical Badarian artifacts for procuring and producing food, adorning their bodies, and expressing their creativity and craftsmanship (Courtesy of the Petrie Museum of Egyptian Archaeology, UCL).

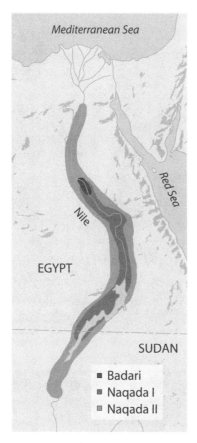

FIGURE 4.6. The approximate extent of the Badari and Naqada I and II cultural regions (by Brenda Coelho).

(a)   (b)

FIGURE 4.7. Naqada I redware (a) and the hallmark Naqada ceramic, (b) black-topped redware (UC10797, UC25787: Copyright of the Petrie Museum of Egyptian Archaeology, UCL).

(a)

(b)

FIGURE 4.8. (a) Example of a Naqada I pot-mark and an abbreviated list of pot-marks (b) recorded on early Naqada vessels. Note how some marks resemble early hieroglyphs (UC10774: Copyright of the Petrie Museum of Egyptian Archaeology, UCL, and Coelho after Brewer 2005, figure 6.8).

(a)

(b)

FIGURE 4.9. Naqada I white cross-lined pottery with geometric designs (a) and (b) dancing (?) human figures (UC15288, UC15339: Copyright of the Petrie Museum of Egyptian Archaeology, UCL).

within particular graves suggests that they might have been a manufacturer's mark or symbols of vessel ownership. A large number of different marks exist, ranging from figurative (humans, animals, boats) to abstract (triangles, crescents, arrows).

The red polished vessels were occasionally decorated with white painted designs (Figure 4.9a, b), comprising geometrical, animal, and vegetal motifs. The fauna represented on the vessels included crocodiles, hippos, and desert

FIGURE 4.10. Interesting artifacts of the Naqada I period are animal relief pots. Figures are molded on the side of the vessel (© The Metropolitan Museum of Art. Image Source: Art Resources, NY).

animals such as scorpions, gazelles, giraffes, and bovids. The human form was also depicted, although with less frequency than animals. In a very significant development, animals were made to stand out from the surface of the vessel in a kind of raised relief decoration (Figure 4.10).

The average Gerzean (Naqada II) burial was a simple pit grave containing a single corpse. Sometimes an inhumation might include two bodies, but rarely more. The corpse was usually found in a fetal position, but the orientation of the body varied from one cemetery to the next. Wrapping of the body in an animal skin was rare; instead, mats or linen cloth was used. Children began to be buried in large pottery vessels (sometimes upturned), and wealthier adults were interred in coffins, which were initially made from basketry, then clay, and finally wood. The switch to rectangular graves for the wealthier classes may be in part attributed to the increased use of coffins. Other changes in burial practices included the placement of funerary offerings farther away from the body, eventually leading to multichambered tombs, one of the basic hallmarks of later Egyptian culture.

Two new types of pottery appeared in the Naqada II period: a rough utilitarian ware sometimes decorated with incised motifs, and a fancier ware with

(a)

(b)

FIGURE 4.11. Naqada II pottery: pink ware with geometric (a) and (b) scenic designs (courtesy of the Oriental Institute of the University of Chicago).

painted decorations or molded handles. The rough ware was made with Nile silt and straw; after firing it acquired a brownish red color. The fancier vessels were tempered with sand instead of straw. When fired at low temperatures, the vessels turned pink, and at higher temperatures, they took on a grayish-green color.

The painted motifs decorating the low-fired pink pots were either geometric or scenic (Figure 4.11a, b). The pots with geometric designs such as spirals, serrated lines, and waves appeared early in the Naqada II period (NII b), whereas scenic designs appeared later (NII c) and continued throughout the period. The scenic designs expressed the basic elements of the Egyptian

FIGURE 4.12. Clay female figurine positioned in a pose very similar to those found on Naqada II pottery (Courtesy of the Brooklyn Museum, http://www.brooklynmuseum.org/).

world: desert and Nile animals, water, trees, and boats. Male human figures were depicted, but only as minor elements within a larger scene; women, on the other hand, dominated some scenes. Female figurines of fired clay are also known from this period but their significance, as with the similarly portrayed females on pottery, remains a mystery (Figure 4.12). High temperature–fired vessels often took the form of the wavy-handled jars made famous by Petrie's classification system.

Concurrent with Upper Egypt's Naqada culture was the Buto-Ma'adi culture of Lower Egypt (Figure 4.13). Unfortunately, comparability to Upper Egyptian ceramics remains problematic: Most Lower Egyptian ceramics come from settlement contexts and Upper Egyptian ceramics from cemeteries. Nevertheless, Friedman's important study of Egyptian settlement ceramics suggests limited contacts between the two Egyptian regions. Although a number of shared pottery attributes exist, it is difficult to ascribe them to borrowing or merely serendipity. Buto-Ma'adi ceramics do, however, have traceable commonalities with Palestine.

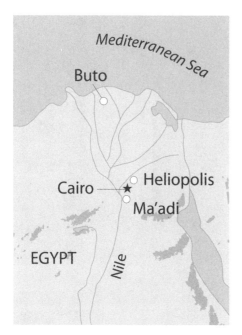

FIGURE 4.13. The sites of Ma'adi, Buto, and Heliopolis, core cultural areas of the Ma'adi-Buto culture of the Delta (by Brenda Coelho).

Typical Ma'adian pottery vessels were globular, with a flat base, a narrow neck, and a flared rim; bottle shapes were also found (Figure 4.14). Ma'adian vessels were rarely decorated but sometimes had marks incised after firing. Like the pot-marks of Upper Egypt, these incisions are poorly understood. Also found were examples of black-topped redware, some clearly imports from Upper Egypt, but others exemplify the Ma'adians' attempt to copy the southern style using local clay. The presence of Palestinian ceramic vessels, most important the wavy-handled vessels that were also copied by the Egyptians, suggests commercial links with that area.

Renee Friedman's detailed analysis of Egyptian domestic ceramics provides one of the only well-documented studies available to compare domestic assemblages of Upper and Lower Egypt. She notes that the Buto-Ma'adi culture seems to have both received and exported certain ceramic attributes associated with its domestic wares. For example, at Buto certain locally produced straw-tempered jars had modeled rims, like those found in Upper Egyptian vessels of the period. Certain types of decorated basins of Lower Egyptian style and manufacture were found in Upper Egypt, underlying the fact that goods and ideas were exchanged in both directions. Utilitarian wares seem most separable, however, by their shape and firing technology. Lower Egyptian

FIGURE 4.14. Ma'adian pottery vessels. Note the lugs and handles, which archaeologists believe helped facilitate their use in long-distance transport from the evolving cultures to the east (photo by D. J. Brewer).

straw-tempered pottery (utilitarian pottery) seems to have been fired under more reducing conditions and at lower temperatures than Upper Egyptian pottery. The preponderance of straw-tempered pottery in Lower Egypt has suggested this technique originated here and filtered to Upper Egypt, but this remains debatable. What clearly occurs, however, is that through time, Upper Egyptian pottery replaces the traditions of that of Lower Egypt.

Flint-working too was local, but influenced by both Upper Egypt and Palestine. Stone vessels carved locally were made from soft stone such as limestone and alabaster, whereas vessels of hard stone such as basalt appear to be imports. Bone and ivory artifacts consisted mainly of needles and punches, although some combs imported from Upper Egypt were found.

Ma'adian burial practices reveal that the deceased were placed in oval pits, in a fetal position, wrapped in a mat or cloth. Originally the bodies did not appear to be oriented in any particular direction, but later they were positioned with the head to the south but facing east, not west, as in Upper Egypt. What is most distinctive about the graves, however, is the near total absence of grave goods: At most one or two pottery vessels might be included. No copper has been found in the burials, but often a Nile clam shell (*Apsatharia rubens*) has been recovered. At other sites, such as Buto and Heliopolis, similar burial customs prevailed. Also evident at these sites was a tendency to copy Upper Egyptian material culture, particularly pottery and its associated Gerzean motifs, as well

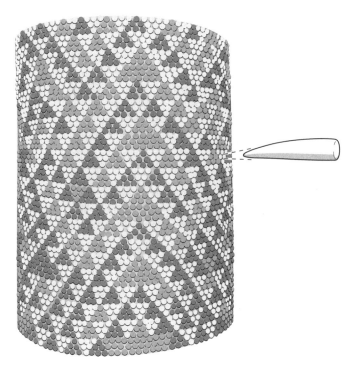

FIGURE 4.15. Clay cone temple reconstruction, showing use of cones in a decorative motif along a column (by Loren Kirkwood after Brewer 2005, figure 6.31).

as the wavy-handled jars. Ma'adi is particularly important, however, because it may have possessed a smelting facility and have traded cast copper objects.

Based on the presence of Upper Egyptian artifacts, three phases have been identified in Ma'adian chronology. The earliest phase coincides with the last half of Naqada I and is best represented by the site of Ma'adi itself. The second phase is identified best with Heliopolis and the earliest levels of Buto, which date to middle Naqada II (i.e., between Naqada II ab and II cd). The final phase, called Dynasty 0, is represented only at Buto.

Buto may have held a particularly advantageous geographical position for a burgeoning sociopolitical system beginning to extend its reach to other developing cultures in the region. Buto's location near the mouth of the Rosetta branch of the Nile and its proximity to the sea (then much closer to the site than today) placed it on a maritime route over which vast quantities of timber, oil, wine, minerals, pottery, and other commodities could be imported and exported. Recent excavations at Buto have recovered clay cones similar to those used to decorate Uruk temples (ca. 3200 BC) in Mesopotamia, offering strong support to the claim of long-distance contacts via the sea (Figure 4.15).

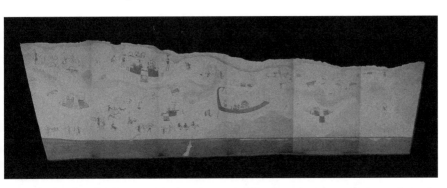

FIGURE 4.16. The wall mural from the famous Lost Tomb (Tomb 100) of Hierakonpolis (Courtesy of the Petrie Museum of Egyptian Archaeology, UCL).

ARCHAEOLOGY, PREDYNASTIC EGYPT, AND SOCIAL COMPLEXITY

During Naqada I and early Naqada II times, Upper Egypt was home to many small, scattered villages. Through time, a number of large population centers became established in both Upper and Lower Egypt. As the general population expanded and a new social and economic order was evolving, so too was an ideological system, which is best exemplified in the growing number of elaborate tombs. Tomb 100 at Hierakonpolis, for example, was a rectangular brick structure measuring 5.85 × 2.85 meters with the floor at a depth of 1.5 meters. The walls were mudbrick covered by a layer of plaster elaborately decorated with Gerzean-style representations, the earliest known example of mural-type tomb painting in Egypt (Figure 4.16).

By 3350 BC local traditions began to merge – sometimes rapidly – into a definable national Egyptian character. Recent work at Abydos in Upper Egypt and Minshat Abu Omar in the Delta has revealed that although Lower and Upper Egypt underwent separate stages of development, by late Naqada II Upper Egyptian culture characteristics were present in the eastern Delta. By the end of the next period, called Naqada III, many of the features of the Dynastic Period are evident. Tombs at Abydos and evidence at Hierakonpolis indicate that these areas were ruled by local chieftain-kings who differentiated themselves from their subjects by using symbols later assumed by the kings of Dynasty 1. Houses at Naqada were arranged along winding streets, indicating a city plan. Ivory tags with proto-hieroglyphs were in use, suggesting that by the end of the Predynastic Period, writing was already established as a means of conveying rank, title, and ownership.

Excavations at Abydos also suggest that at the end of the Naqada period, the cultural unification of Upper and Lower Egypt had begun and may have culminated with the legendary unification of Egypt at Dynasty 0 (ca: 3050 BC). By this time, both Egypt's northern and southern sections exhibited what before had been a typically Upper Egyptian material culture, attesting to the gradual cultural domination of the north by the south.

What does this say about Egypt's contribution to the general understanding of society's rise to sociopolitical complexity? It is clear that during the Naqada period, Egypt journeyed from egalitarian village to the brink of state-level complexity. With respect to Egypt's journey, probably every major theoretical approach has been applied at one time or another in an attempt to explain aspects of this great transition, from Marxist to Jungianism to modern ethnic interpretations. Yet each attempt has failed to be accepted by some significant faction of archaeologists. We might ask then: Why do we continue to seek an answer to this problem? We do so because answering it reveals something about ourselves.

5

UNIFICATION AND THE KING: THE LIMITS
OF ARCHAEOLOGY

The late Predynastic, Naqada III culture is best typified by the concentration of economic and political power into the hands of fewer and fewer individuals, a process that began in Naqada II times but intensified in the final 200 years prior to the First Dynasty. Naqada III is divided into two parts, Naqada IIIa and IIIb with the latter often referred to as the Protodynastic or Dynasty 0. This final period, lasting only about 100 years, marks the transition between the old Predynastic order and the new Dynastic civilization distinguished by the presence of a king, later to be known as Pharaoh, who stood over a centralized bureaucracy governing the Nile Valley from Aswan to the Mediterranean Sea. How the peoples of the Nile Valley unified and Egypt's first king came to power continues to intrigue archaeologists.

According to Egyptian tradition, Menes, King of Upper Egypt, founded the First Dynasty and built the capital city of Memphis, but nowhere does it say that Menes actually unified the country.

> ... the first royal house numbers eight kings, the first of whom Menes of This reigned for 62 years. He was carried off by a hippopotamus and perished. [Africanus (Manetho Fr. 60)]

> The King called [Menes} reigned for 60 years. He made a foreign expedition and won renown but was carried off by a hippopotamus [Eusebius (Manetho Fr. 7)]

> The priests told me that Menes was the first king of Egypt and that first he separated Memphis from the Nile by a dam. . . . Then, when this first king (Menes) had made what he thus cut off to be dry land, he first founded in it that city which is now called Memphis. (Herodotus II: 99).

As discussed in the previous chapter, archaeology and the objects it retrieves and studies is unfortunately not well suited to answer questions dealing with specific events in time, its forte being the study of processes over time. Even the more generalized goals that archaeology achieves require a series of parallel inquiries from scholars with differing backgrounds, combining their information and formulating a working hypothesis or model to account for the data.

How then has archaeology worked to solve questions such as Egypt's unification or the rise of its first king? As practiced, archaeology is a collage of theory, methods, and techniques borrowed from disciplines as far ranging as art and physics, and these seemingly disparate disciplines have aligned to solve archaeological problems.

According to the ancient Egyptians, there were originally two kingdoms: a kingdom of Upper Egypt and a kingdom of Lower Egypt. An Upper Egyptian king through force of arms conquered Lower Egypt and unified the Nile Valley under his leadership. But, is this version of Egyptian prehistory true? Were there two kingdoms, and did Menes have anything to do with unifying Egypt or, more to the point, was there ever a Menes?

Social anthropologists tell us that governance over a large region requires a large population with a diversity of craft specialists and agriculturalists, a center from which authority can be extended, and a financial powerbase from which to pay for the services a leader requires. During the Naqada III period, there were several population centers of sufficient size and wealth to have served as regional centers, with a socially stratified populace engaged in agriculture, craft production, and trade. Such centers by their very nature would have required a central form of leadership to make decisions on behalf of and for the benefit of the community, and this leader (or leaders) would eventually come to control considerable resources. Hierakonpolis and Abydos in Upper Egypt certainly fit these conditions, as does Buto in the Delta.

It is at Hierakonpolis and Abydos where artifacts purported "to document" the unification of Egypt and to identify its first king have been recovered. Unfortunately some of the most intriguing artifacts relating to Egypt's origins are tainted by the aura of "careless archaeology." This unfortunate label falls on James Quibell and Frederick Green, whose work at Hierakonpolis created as many questions as answers.

The ancient site of Hierakonpolis has only recently received the attention it deserves. Work conducted at the site from its beginnings in the late nineteenth century until today has done much to shape our view of Predynastic Egypt. In 1897 and 1899, Quibell and Green first undertook work at the site for Petrie's Egyptian Research Account. Already by this time, the site and the cemetery in particular had been heavily plundered by looters and local farmers (*sebakhin*) who would remove the mineral-rich soil and transport it to their fields. After some disappointing work salvaging artifacts from the plundered gravesites, Quibell and Green turned their attention to the ancient town of Nekhen and its temple remains.

The temple was not hard to find: Throughout the Dynastic period the temple had been built and rebuilt to commemorate the birthplace of Horus, the mythical first earthly king of Egypt. Within the temple area the excavations revealed traces of a circular sand platform surrounded by a retaining wall of Predynastic age. Excavating near the center of the sand mound, Quibell and Green discovered intrusive deposits of a later Old Kingdom chapel and, "there came into view a hawk of thin copper plate, with head and plumes of gold" (Quibell 1899: 27). The vision did not last as the copper immediately disintegrated but the gold head and plume remained intact; this is one of the finest pieces of ancient gold work from this period.

Further work revealed a life-size copper statue of a king, and on its chest lay a crumpled sheet of copper with the embossed inscription of Pepi I. Back at their living quarters and lab (a conveniently located tomb), Quibell and Green found a second smaller figure within while cleaning out the hollow trunk of the statue. The method of construction of both was the same. Apparently the copper sheets had been formed over a wooden core and nailed into position, the core having long since decomposed. Both figures, deliberately dismantled at the time of burial, were thought to be of the same king.

Buried with the copper statues were two other items: a ceramic lion and the statue of a seated king carved in green stone and inscribed with the name of Horus Khasekhem, last ruler of the Second Dynasty. On the base of the statue is a record of kills: 47,209 Lower Egyptian rebels.

The next astounding discovery was made in very uncertain circumstances, between two walls of the Dynastic temple. It was very clear that the objects in what the excavators called the "Main Deposit" were potentially very important (Figure 5.1). Although Quibell and Green took great care in their removal and cataloguing, their excavation records do not denote exactly where they were found.

The Main Deposit was said to have "probably" been found atop a dark stratum of rich, charcoal-laden soil dated by pottery to the Late Predynastic–Early Dynastic period. All we know about the Narmer Palette, one of the most important artifacts ever recovered, is that it was found near the Main Deposit. From Green's field notes (Quibell kept none), it seems to have been found a meter or two from the Main Deposit, but in a 1902 publication, Green notes that it came from the same level as the Main Deposit. Quibell too believes it was contemporary with the Main Deposit. Clearly, issues surrounding the excavation procedures and artifact provenience have made our search for Egypt's beginnings more challenging.

EXCAVATION

Excavation is intimately linked with the science of archaeology, and it is the most demanding in terms of costs, physical exertion, and patience. Any loss of information on any object might become critical at some time in the future – a problem we now face with the Narmer Palette.

Excavation is the exposing, processing, and recording of archaeological remains systematically recovered from buried contexts. It adheres to the Laws of Superposition and involves removal of sediments in the reverse order to the way they were laid down, gradually revealing each successive stage in the history of a site. This seems like a simple enough task, but in reality it is an extremely difficult puzzle of ancient floors, hearths, trenches, walls, and other intrusive deposits from later activities. Because the site, once excavated, is essentially destroyed, it is referred to as a destructive technique, and therefore great care is taken to record all aspects of the work with the goal, theoretically, to be able to reconstruct the site from the notes and measurements.

Artifact context (physical location) is everything. It is the relationship of artifacts to one another and to the depositional unit within which an artifact was found that ascribes interpretive meaning to the object. By separating a site into basic, discrete units, archaeologists are able to view a specific period of site history. By reconstituting the site in three dimensions, it can be viewed through time. Without artifact provenience, the site is nothing but a hole in the ground and the recovered objects no more than pieces of shelf-art.

Archaeological excavation is one of those things that can only be learned and appreciated through practice. Once experience has been gained, most will adhere to the long-held adage that it is a lot more fun to talk about digging than it is to do it, as it means long hours in unbearable heat, fending off bloodthirsty insects, removing slithering reptiles and scorpions from one's pit, consuming bad food, drinking unreliable water, and always wondering if the vehicle will break down on the way back to the home-camp.

Like a survey, excavation is based on a predetermined plan designed to answer the archaeologist's specific questions. Where one digs can be based on intuition, on site history, or on a sampling design. Prior to any digging, a map of the study area is made, the site or area of interest is gridded, and the surface

FIGURE 5.1. Part of the artifact cache from the "Main Deposit" as recorded by the excavators (Courtesy of the Petrie Museum of Egyptian Archaeology, UCL).

prepared for excavation. Often a test trench or "sondage" is made to provide basic information about subsurface materials and conditions, depth and type of cultural materials, stratigraphy, and other important details excavators are likely to be concerned about.

Excavation units vary in size depending on what problem the archaeologist seeks to solve: If architecture, then a 10 × 10 meter unit might be appropriate; if the archaeologist seeks small Paleolithic tools and their juxtaposition to microstratigraphy is important, a 2 × 2 or even 1 × 1 meter square is used. The smaller the unit size, the more precise the provenience, but the longer it takes to remove a given unit of earth.

The golden rule of excavation is to work from the known to the unknown and always horizontally. Uncover each layer of earth carefully before moving into the unit below. Although depositional units are usually based on stratigraphy, significant artifact changes can occur within a single depositional episode. The exact provenience of each artifact is plotted on the unit's level map and its depth measured from a datum (usually a corner stake of known elevation); soil samples and other organic materials are also collected and labeled for study. Non-portable artifacts (features) might include fire hearths or post-holes and walls. Horizontal plan drawings are made at the interface of every excavated sedimentary unit (Figure 5.2a), with the location of all artifacts and other important natural phenomena located within the plan and their depth noted. A profile drawing of the excavation unit, as well as the entire site profile, is also made for cross-referencing (Figure 5.2b). Further detail is added from the excavation notes, where entries record subtle differences in soil, inferences about artifact provenience, and other information the excavator deems important to impart about the excavation procedure and finds. Used as complementary parts of the excavation archive, the final product, the notes and plans and recovered artifacts, allow the site to be reconstructed in three dimensions, detailing the physical relationships between stratigraphy and artifacts. Clearly, excavation is composed of a little digging and a lot of measuring and note taking.

RECTIFYING THE ERROR: THE MAIN DEPOSIT

Using information from modern excavations, Günter Dreyer, the late Barbara Adams, and others have attempted to reconcile Quibell and Green's descriptions with recent published reports of Hierakonpolis excavations. In sum, Quibell and Green note four stratigraphic units that have been corroborated by recent work. The earliest is Naqada II in date. The second stratum correlates with the early sand mound and temple revetment discovered prior to the uncovering of the Old Kingdom treasures. Based on the types of broken pottery recovered from this level, the conclusion is that it appears to date between Naqada II and III. The third stratum described by Quibell and Green was a dark, charcoal-discolored level lying below the Old Kingdom Temple; it was dated, based on pottery, to Dynasty 0–1. The fourth level was thought to be Dynasty 1–3 in age.

Without corroborating documentation, the Main Deposit of artifacts could have come from any period between Naqada II to Dynasty 3 times; Green states only that the Main Deposit "in all probability" comes from level 3, a Dynasty 0–1 unit. Nevertheless, following Quibell and Green's notes and published reports, Dreyer believes he can further refine the location of the Main Deposit to an area below the northeast sector of the Old Kingdom temple, atop the third level. The original location of the Narmer Palette, unfortunately, remains questionable.

What is so important about the artifacts that we look back into Quibell and Green's field notes for answers? This group of artifacts is thought to be an offering buried in the corner foundation of the temple – a relatively common practice in ancient Egypt. The ancient cache included over 200 objects, arguably the most important being the Narmer and Scorpion mace

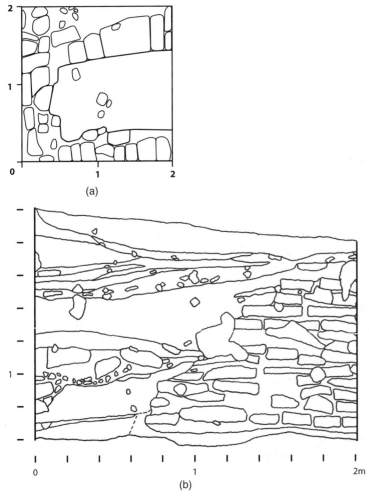

FIGURE 5.2. An excavation horizontal plan (a) and excavation profile (b) from the Delta site of Kom el-Hisn (Ault and Flores after Wenke et al. 1988, figure 5).

heads and the Narmer Palette. Because they represent some of the earliest examples of Egyptian glyptic evidence ever found, their precise provenience is of extreme importance, in particular the Narmer Palette, which depicts a southern king defeating the north and claiming rule over all of Egypt.

With exact provenience in doubt, we must look beyond archaeology to interpret and date the palette. All told, there are some twenty known ceremonial palettes similar to the famous Narmer Palette. Many are only fragments but about a dozen are complete enough that they can be possibly interpreted and used as sources of information about their period of manufacture.

Philologist and art historian Hermann Ranke has divided the palettes into two groups that he believes reflect a simple chronology. The first group is composed of images, which are all roughly the same size and scattered over the surface of the palette without any apparent organization or hieroglyphic signs. In the second group of palettes, space was divided into horizontal lines (registers), and early forms of hieroglyphs are present. The Hunter's palette may date in between the groups, with two glyph-like symbols, perhaps representing nomes of the east and west Delta, and hunters organized in rows but not anchored to a register. The Narmer Palette, the most complete and most internally organized of the extant palettes, probably postdates the two palette groups and the Hunters palette and reflects a Protodynastic date (Figure 5.3).

The Narmer Palette (Figure 5.4) honors the exploits of King Narmer and presumably his prowess in combat. At the top on either side of the palette is the king's name within a *serekh*; it is framed on both sides by the benevolent cow goddess, Bat. *Serekh* was an Egyptian word that meant "to make known." It was a paneled rectangle surrounding the king's name – a design meant to represent the paneled or niched façade of the palace and royal tomb.

The earliest *serekh*s lacked inscriptions but were often surmounted by double falcons. These were followed by *serekh*s that featured the rulers Ka and Narmer, and finally a third group of *serekh*s featuring Aha, thus establishing a sequence of rulers that is corroborated by archaeological excavations at Abydos, where the tombs of most of these leaders are located (Figure 5.5).

On one side of the palette, Narmer is shown wearing the *deshret*, what will later become the characteristic headgear of the Pharaoh as King of Lower Egypt. The king is preceded by his priest and four standard-bearers carrying fetishes; his sandal-bearer and foot washer bring up the rear of the precession. His entourage inspects rows of corpses with bound arms and severed heads. The place of slaughter is identified from the glyphs above the bodies as a Delta city, possibly Buto. The central register of this highly organized design shows a circular depression, around which are two four-legged creatures with intertwined serpent-like necks. This foreign-inspired character has been interpreted as a theme of union, Narmer being responsible for joining the Upper and Lower kingdoms into one. At the bottom of the palette the king, symbolized as a "strong bull," breaks down a fortified township and tramples a foreigner, identified as a Delta dweller or perhaps a Libyan.

The reverse side of the palette shows Narmer, accompanied by his sandal-bearer, wearing the white crown, the *hedjet*, which was to become the emblematic headgear of the Pharaoh as King of Upper Egypt. The king is shown

GROUP I

DOG'S PALETTE
Height=42.5 cm

BATTLEFIELD PALETTE
(VULTURES)
Height=32.8 cm

HUNTER'S PALETTE
Height=66.8 cm

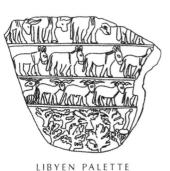

GROUP II

LIBYEN PALETTE
Height=18.5 cm

NARMER PALETTE
Height=63.5 cm

FIGURE 5.3. An example of Ranke's chronological placement of palettes based on style and internal arrangement (Jackie Gardner after Petrie 1953, pls. D, F and G19; Quibell 1898, pl. XII; Smith 1949, figure 25).

(a)   (b)

FIGURE 5.4. (a) and (b) The Narmer Palette (Werner Forman/ Art Resource, NY, Egyptian Museum, Cairo).

clubbing a submissive enemy with a pear-shaped mace in a pose that becomes engrained in Dynastic art and can be found on commemorative works for the next three millennia. Above the victim are hieroglyphic symbols that read "domain of the harpoon," which in later periods is a reference to a district of the Delta. Another reference to the Delta can be found above the hieroglyphs where the head of a defeated enemy is situated within a thicket of six papyrus plants. A falcon leads the tethered enemy by the nose, as one would lead a subjugated farm animal. The message that the king has subdued the enemy seems quite clear. Because Narmer appears here as the King of both Upper and Lower Egypt, he has been equated with the semi-legendary Menes. Another important artifact, the Narmer Mace Head, also seems to corroborate his rule over the Delta. Here, the king is shown seated on a dais receiving gifts, wearing the *deshret* crown.

Further evidence seemingly corroborating Narmer as the ruler of a unified Egypt came in 1977, when the German archaeologist Günter Dreyer, clearing around the tomb of Narmer, found a small ivory label. On it the name of Narmer, the catfish, was evident, and the figure of Narmer was shown smiting an enemy, out of whose head sprouts a papyrus plant (Figure 5.6).

FIGURE 5.5. *Serekhs* in chronological order (top to bottom) (Brenda Coelho after Kaiser and Dryer 1982, Ab. 14).

FIGURE 5.6. Artists reproduction of the ivory label of Narmer, showing his triumph over a northern (Delta?) enemy (Ault and Flores after Dryer et al. 1998, Figure 29).

This discovery relays the same message as the Narmer Palette: the conquest over a Delta (or Asiatic?) enemy. This third piece of evidence would seem to solidify Narmer as Egypt's unifier, but evidence to the contrary has also surfaced. A *serekh* of Ka found on a cylinder seal from the site of Tarkhan and other inscriptions from Abydos refer to revenue received by the royal treasury, suggesting that a functioning centralized economy existed prior to Narmer's reign. Some even argue that a shadowy earlier figure known as King Scorpion also ruled a united Egypt.

King Scorpion, who predated Narmer by several generations, is poorly known in Egyptian history. The famous Scorpion Mace Head, part of the Main Deposit find at Hierakonpolis, shows a king, identified as Scorpion, wearing the white crown of Upper Egypt, standing triumphantly over a canal with a hoe in hand, probably commemorating the success of an irrigation project (Figure 5.7). Plants characteristic of Lower Egypt can also be seen, suggesting he had some authority over this region. The reverse side of the mace head is unfortunately destroyed. Recent discoveries at Abydos, however, suggest that the scorpion sign found on this piece is a title, not a name, and thus King Scorpion may not be the proper designation for the individual. Nevertheless, his real-life counterpart, whoever he might have been, may have ruled in some sense over parts of both Upper and Lower Egypt.

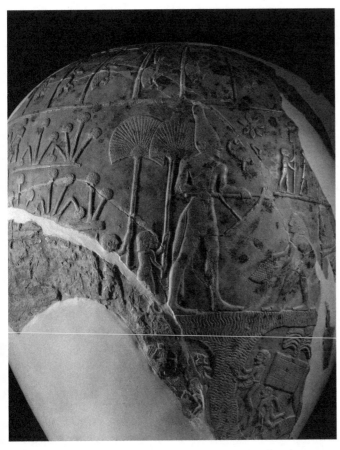

FIGURE 5.7. The Scorpion Macehead (Werner Forman/Art Resource, NY, Ashmolean Museum, Oxford).

By Egyptian accounts the kings of the first two dynasties all came from a place called This. Although This has never been located, the mortuary complex associated with the settlement was most likely Abydos, the burial place of Egypt's first kings and in all likelihood their immediate predecessors.

Cylinder seals and engraved tags are two other sources of corroborative evidence that help clarify the identity and succession of the early rulers. Cylinder seals (Figure 5.8) first appeared in Egypt in Naqada II as imports from Mesopotamia. These were copied by the Egyptians, who like their eastern neighbors used them as a means of labeling mud seals and stoppers on pottery jars. One seal dated to about 3000 BC lists the first five kings of Egypt in sequential order (Figure 5.9).

Engraved tags of ivory, bone, and ebony have provided additional information (Figure 5.10). These were generally used for everyday purposes such

FIGURE 5.8. An early Naqada Period cylinder seal (UC10799: Copyright of the Petrie Museum of Egyptian Archaeology, UCL).

as defining ownership of funerary equipment or listing the vintage or source of a wine or oil, but they also chronicled important events that occurred in a given year – a method of dating the passage of years.

Günter Dreyer initially began investigating the Abydos cemeteries to reclaim what might have been lost from earlier excavations, and his efforts revealed some forty engraved tags found at one large tomb (U-j) (Figure 5.11). The aforementioned tag depicting Narmer vanquishing a Delta adversary was part of this cache. What was also interesting about the tags was that some gave regions in the Delta as sources of origin, suggesting that some commodities arrived at Abydos as taxes from Lower Egypt. If so, this would suggest that at least parts of the Delta were already under control of an Upper Egyptian leader

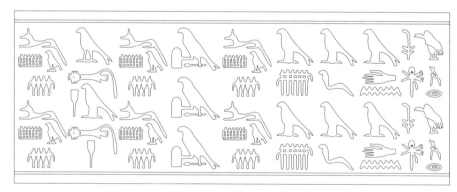

FIGURE 5.9. Impression on a cylinder seal listing the first five kings of Egypt (Brenda Coelho after Spencer 1993, figure 43).

FIGURE 5.10. Example of a well-preserved Dynasty 1 ivory from the reign of Djet (Courtesy of the Oriental Institute of the University of Chicago).

FIGURE 5.11. Tomb U-j where a cache of tags and labels was found. (Courtesy of Günter Dreyer, German Archaeological Institute, Cairo).

prior to Narmer's rule. Another interesting find in U-j was a large-model ivory *heka* scepter, an essential part of Egyptian royal regalia, which was evidently in use at least 200 years before the first king ascended to the throne.

U-j is the largest tomb (ca. 9.1 × 7.3 meters) in Cemetery U, an area adjacent to the early Dynastic graves of Abydos. The brick lining of the walls has survived, as well as wood, matting, and brick from the roof superstructure. The tomb contained hundreds of Egyptian wavy-handled pottery vessels as well as beer jars, bread molds, and plates dating to the Naqada IIIa2 phase (ca. 3200 BC). Many of the Egyptian vessels bear inscriptions in black ink, including depictions of a scorpion. One chamber of the tomb was filled with about 400 Palestinian-style (wine?) vessels.

Who was buried at U-j? The conclusion based on the name found on many pottery vessels is that it was a person called Scorpion, but not necessarily the King Scorpion of Hierakonpolis fame. There are other names recorded in the tomb as well, simple names written with animal signs, such as dog or lion, or seashell. Perhaps, as some have hypothesized, the names represent members of a kingly line predating the First Dynasty that ruled over a late Predynastic Egypt.

By analyzing the *serekhs*, tags, seal impressions, and fragments of inscribed pottery, archaeologists have identified the Abydos tombs thought to belong to King Narmer and his immediate predecessors, kings Aha, Iry-Hor and Ka. The distribution of burials at Abydos and the evolution of the tombs' complexity provide a clear sign of continuity between the Late Predynastic and Early Dynastic rulers. The sum of all the collected evidence suggests, however, that Narmer perhaps was not the first to rule over parts of the Delta or even to claim rule over all of Egypt.

Viewing the issue of rulership from the Delta, Buto would be the counterpart of Upper Egypt's bustling settlements of Naqada, Abydos, and Hierakonpolis. With due diligence, a German team led by Thomas von der Way and Dina Faltings were able to excavate (with the help of water pumps) deep into Buto's prehistory to its earliest levels, some 7 meters below the modern surface.

Seven major depositional episodes have been identified at Buto dating from Dynastic times back to Naqada IIb. The stratified accumulation of debris, mostly hundreds of thousands of potsherds, has allowed Faltings to study Buto culture through time. The first two units represent Naqada IIb and IIcd, and finds can be easily placed within the established Buto-Ma'adi culture, but the third level, referred to as a "transitional" level and dated to Naqada IId1 and IId2, is characterized by an increasing amount of pottery made in the Upper Egyptian tradition, based on their shape and manufacturing technique.

Through her analysis of the pottery Faltings also was able to identify a number of Negev-like ceramics.

Buto pottery was made using the slab technique, making it discernible from the pottery of Upper Egypt or the Negev. Buto potters mixed Nile clay with straw or flax, and from a lump of clay that served as the bottom of the vessel, they attached slabs of clay, then squeezed it all together to make a pot. After the clay dried, its surface was burnished with a pebble to make it more watertight. Interestingly, as soon as pottery from Upper Egypt appeared, it seems to have been favored.

A makeshift pottery kiln was found at Buto, showing that Buto potters tried to first copy the Upper Egyptian styles using their own local materials and techniques, but after 3100 BC, the indigenous Delta pottery vanishes, being replaced almost completely by Upper Egyptian vessels. Concurrent with the transitional phase in ceramics, mudbrick structures appear among the traditional pole-supported thatched homes. This has been interpreted by some as evidence that Upper Egyptians were living at Buto. Also noted was an increase in grave goods in some, presumably, elite burials. Based on this evidence, von der Way believes that the rise of Upper Egyptian influence was an economical one and peaceful overall.

Work at Minshat Abu Omar (Figure 5.12), a site that spans the Predynastic to Early Dynastic periods, has provided further detail to the transitional period noted at Buto's level 3. Excavation leaders Dieter Wildung and Karla Kroeper note that even though the burial goods progressively take on a more Upper Egyptian character, with goods of Upper Egyptian manufacture increasing during this period, no weaponry has been found with the interred. This they believe represents a peaceful economic transitional period rather than one carried out through force of arms. Studies of the human remains, too, have produced no strong evidence of an increase in violent death associated with the transitional period or the period shortly following, the time when unification is thought to have occurred.

In the northeast Delta a Dutch survey has located a number of Predynastic sites. Two sites in particular, Tell Ibrahim Awad and Tell el-Iswid, span the pre- and post-introduction of Upper Egyptian material goods. At Tel Ibrahim Awad the stratigraphy shows an uninterrupted sequence from late Predynastic to Early Dynastic. The earliest phase is dated to Naqada IIcd and does not contain brick architecture, the settlement being represented by postholes for wickerwork huts, numerous hearths, and clay-lined storage pits. In the second phase, contemporary with Naqada III, the remains of rectangular mudbrick buildings were found. The pottery of the earlier phase is comparable to the straw-tempered pottery from Buto. As with Buto, the straw pottery is replaced by Naqada wares in the second phase (Naqada III). The early phase at Tell el-Iswid is dominated by ceramics of the Delta tradition too, although a few Upper Egyptian examples do exist. The second phase falls completely within the Upper Egyptian pottery traditions. A change from wicker and pole huts to mudbrick architecture also occurs at Tell el-Iswid during this transitional period. A similar phenomenon has been noted at other Delta sites as well: Tell el-Ginn, el-Husseiniya, Tell Samara, Gerzia Sangaha, Kufur Nigm, Beni Amir, el-Beida, and Bubastis. Nowhere does it seem that this cultural shift was accompanied by violence.

Given that Buto is one of the most northerly of Delta sites, one might expect earlier examples of Upper Egyptian culture in more southerly Delta communities, and perhaps it is in these areas that violence occurred. Unfortunately, there exists a 200-kilometer stretch of the Nile void of any significant cultural deposits for this period. The site of Ma'adi, located at the juncture of the Delta and Nile proper, does little to elaborate on the transitional phase.

Further south, the sites of Harageh and Sedment, directly east of the Fayum, although producing only limited quantities of pottery, did fit into the Delta tradition prior to Naqada IIc times. The neighboring site of Abusir el-Melek, dating slightly later (Naqada IIcd–III), exhibits an interesting blend of the two material cultures. Over 900 graves were excavated with most of the interments being described as moderately affluent. The simplest graves were oval pits, but a number of large elaborate burials were found as well. These were rectangular, lined with mudbrick, and contained wooden or ceramic coffins. A few of the graves were divided into rectangular rooms, each containing typical grave goods of the period. Interestingly, more than one of the richly furnished tombs belonged to children. A child would not have had the opportunity to amass such prestige through deeds, so wealth and status must have been conferred upon them through heredity. Simply put, these burials were the children of important leaders in a socially stratified community.

The pottery found in these graves was a curious mix of Upper and Lower Egyptian traditions. Much of the pottery could be associated with Upper Egypt traditions, but the graves lacked black-topped redware. Instead they had a number of black-polished wares typical of Lower Egypt. Flint tools, pear-shaped mace heads, cosmetic palettes, combs, and bone pins were copies of southern forms. Whether el-Melek was an Upper Egyptian community with some Lower Egyptian traits or vice versa is difficult to say without corroborating evidence, but again there does not seem to be any evidence of violence.

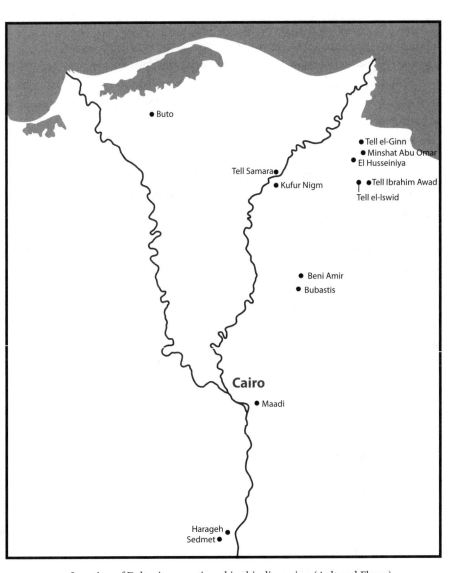

FIGURE 5.12. Location of Delta sites mentioned in this discussion (Ault and Flores).

ADDRESSING THE ARCHAEOLOGICAL QUESTION

How did Egypt transform itself from a collage of regionally governed centers to a unified state under a single king? By reviewing the evidence we find that at Buto, as well as other Delta sites, the amount of Lower Egyptian ceramic vessels and lithics gradually decreases in favor of Upper Egyptian types from the second half of Naqada II (d2), being totally replaced by Naqada III. Similar changes can also be detected in the building methods of tombs and houses. There is no hiatus in the archaeological record suggesting abandonment or destruction between the levels represented by dissimilar artifacts. The combined evidence from all Delta sites suggests that the transition occurred without violence and with the inhabitants carrying on their regular activities: a condition quite contrary to many scenes depicted on commemorative objects.

Given the archaeological evidence, what do we make of the Narmer Palette, where clearly the message is that King Narmer has conquered districts of the Delta and claims rulership of both north and south?

Numerous Predynastic palettes have been found that portray victory over a natural or human enemy. From this point of view, the Narmer Palette perhaps simply provides evidence of smiting Lower Egypt, a feat repeated by rulers from Scorpion to Dynasty 2's King Khasekhemui. In other words, it may simply be the first known example of a violent means of expressing a process that had already taken place in earlier times. The numerous pieces of evidence suggesting the Delta or parts thereof were paying taxes to Upper Egypt prior to Narmer's reign underscores this point. The assimilation of the Delta into southern Naqada culture may have occurred at several historical junctions, but was finally immortalized by the Narmer Palette.

Thus Menes, or his real-life equivalent, probably never existed, at least as the individual responsible for all the attributed feats. Rather he is most likely a compilation of several individuals whose deeds were recorded through oral tradition and identified as the work of a single person, thereby creating a central hero figure for Egypt's unification. As with the personalities of the Bible, Menes was part fiction, part truth, and the years have masked the boundaries, creating a legend of unification. Even his death is apocryphal, having been devoured and carried away by a hippopotamus.

If territorial expansion, unity, and disunity occurred a number of times, then why and how did a centralized Egypt finally become permanent? It is quite certain from archaeological evidence that Naqada III Egyptians in some of the larger population centers were in contact with cultures to the east, south, and west. That the Egyptians were impressed with the developing states of Mesopotamia, however, seems clear from their borrowing of eastern motifs seen in early Egyptian art. The most classic example of these is the Narmer and Hunters' palettes. Equally clear is that this interaction coincided with the rise of Egypt's Dynastic civilization. The role of foreign contacts and their potential contribution has been seen as a prime mover to social complexity and nation building for some time, but it was not the sole catalyst.

When all the evidence for change in the Predynastic is reviewed, we can see a number of things occurring almost simultaneously: environmental change, population shifts, advances in irrigation technology, grain storage and redistribution, influx of ideas from foreign lands – and other stimuli that we may never know. These stimuli had to be addressed in some manner, and a centralized government was the result. The ruler of such a group, either benignly and perhaps on occasion by force, organized the growing population so that it could be effectively directed to support public works and the administrative offices needed to run them.

From Late Naqada II (Naqada IIcd) onward, it is possible that powerful regional rulers were occasionally able to bring together large populations and territory under their control. The territory and communities they influenced probably waxed and waned through the generations, until finally individuals with sufficient power and charisma brought greater amounts of territory under their control and commemorated these events symbolically through the artifacts we have recovered. That is, they were able to combine actual rulership with the symbols of rulership that we recognize today as royal symbols of the Dynastic kings.

As many of the inscribed tags suggest, by the middle of the Naqada III Period, many of the administrative offices needed to control the economic and agricultural aspects of the countryside were in place. In essence, all the elements of the Dynastic civilization had been achieved except the unification of Egypt under a single ruler.

The influx of foreign ideas, goods, and services presented an opportunity for some local rulers to take a central role in cultural exchanges, eventually amassing tremendous wealth (by evidence of their tombs) and the power that derives from such wealth. Gaining control over ports of entry eventually became a goal of some provincial rulers: Control of trade meant wealth and power, which could be translated into political alliances.

Archaeological research suggests that unification was gained predominantly through economic means rather than physical combat. That is, through time, we find Lower Egypt first emulating certain types of pottery and cultural traditions that historically belonged to Upper Egypt, and later fully adopting Upper Egyptian traditions and material goods. It was a voluntary adoption that simply engulfed the Delta cultures to such a point that their own traditions were abandoned in favor of those from Upper Egypt. The people of the Nile Valley then accepted the new political regime and its ruler, ushering in the first great territorial nation. To be sure, some areas resisted and were forcibly annexed, and to a new king showing off his prowess, these are the episodes that would be chosen to be portrayed in commemorative objects.

Because writing had yet to reach its full potential, oral history relayed the story of unification; as with all stories, this history was made entertaining through the adventures of heroes, particularly the king, whose exploits in combat and other examples of royal prowess were emphasized. These stories were eventually recorded in written form, parts of which have come down to us. It also must be remembered that these stories, in essence, served as propaganda designed to unify a people rather than to present accurate information. Beyond the territory brought under political control lay a vast and complex society that also had to adjust to this new order of government and accept the king as ruler. Through aggrandizement, the king took on the air of a god on earth and was accorded the respect and trust of the populace.

Thus archaeology, aided by parallel lines of evidence from studies in iconography, architecture, art history, ceramic studies, and carbon dating to name but a few, is able to recreate 5000-year-old events that occurred within a 100–200-year period, but we really have not been able to explain why those events happened. We have only "described" what may have occurred; the reasons they happened remain elusive. For all archaeology has done to uncover Egypt's past, the lack of a fully bona fide body of theory has left some of the most intriguing questions unanswered and perhaps unanswerable.

6

THE FIRST GREAT CYCLE: HYPOTHESES AND MODELS

Traditionally, the Early Dynastic (Dynasty 1–2) and Old Kingdom (Dynasty 3–6) periods are treated as separate historical units. Archaeologically, however, these two periods represent a continuum from the beginning of the socially complex state of Egypt, established around 3050 BC, to its collapse at the end of the Sixth Dynasty (ca. 2181 BC). It is in this first great cycle of Egyptian civilization that we see the development of monumental stone architecture, writing, imperialistic trade networking, and the rise of an immensely intricate sociopolitical bureaucracy. The massive monuments of the day, most notably the huge pyramid complexes constructed to honor the memory of the deceased kings of the era, provide clear evidence of the vitality of Egypt's early state.

Unfortunately, we know remarkably little about how the state was actually run – how the vast hinterland articulated with the central government, how taxes were collected and redistributed from the government treasuries, or even how autonomous or dependent each region was to the central authority – and it is here that archaeology is trying to make inroads into what has traditionally been the realm of philologists, epigraphers, and historians.

Granted, deciphering of texts and tomb scenes can be done independently of artifact provenience, but archaeological context can enhance the value of translations as well as offer new insights. For example, in Asia Minor where considerably more effort has been placed on understanding the inner workings of sociopolitical systems, archaeological excavations have brought to light important evidence related to urban political organization from a most unlikely place: inscriptions found on theatre seats. Although the inscriptions were translated in a lab, their provenience added important information. The inscriptions were family or clan names and represented voting tribes on an urban council: The theatre was in fact an assembly hall.

Because of the care taken by the archaeologists in recording the exact location of every find, they were able to discern how many clans made up the council and the size of the voting body. In fact, the juxtaposition of the named seats may even offer clues to ancient alliances, but only because of careful archaeological practices were they even able to speculate about these issues.

Changing the scale from assembly hall seats to settlements, understanding how individual communities were articulated within a larger social context has significance for determining the way Early Dynastic and Old Kingdom Egypt was organized. Unfortunately, as archaeologist Barry Kemp noted, even after more than a century of excavation, evidence for the nature and distribution of early settlements in Egypt remains sparse and unsatisfactory.

As with all early complex societies the Egyptian state structure developed out of existing settlements, their distribution across the landscape, and changing political and economic forces. The extent to which these elements influenced Egypt's developmental trajectory has been the subject of much discussion but unfortunately, little actual archaeology. Based on current knowledge, the general consensus seems to be that the character of Dynastic Egypt owes its existence to a complex set of factors involving geography, the agricultural potential of the Nile Valley, Predynastic political structures, and the general cultural milieu of the Near East – not a particularly profound statement given that the same could be said of any culture from any geographic region.

In the absence of extensive archaeological data, scholars have relied upon epigraphic sources, regional surveys, and small test excavations to build a picture of a largely rural Egypt with little of the highly urbanized character of Mesopotamia and its city-states. In fact, some scholars of the 1960s viewed Egypt as an anachronism: a civilization without cities. But is this true? Egypt certainly had large population centers such as Memphis, Hierakonpolis, and Abydos, but how they and other centers functioned within the state remains a subject of archaeological inquiry.

ARCHAEOLOGICAL QUESTIONS, THEORIES, AND HYPOTHESES

How an archaeologist "explains" a group of artifacts is as varied as the discipline itself. What is considered an explanation depends in no small way on the practitioner's paradigm (see Chapter 1). For example, explaining a plague of locusts on Egypt's crops from the perspective of a medieval theological paradigm, one might conclude that God's wrath was invoked due to a lack of faith by Pharaoh. A different paradigm might explain the same event as due to a behavioral change brought about by increased population densities, whereby a normally solitary species of grasshopper underwent a phase change and became gregarious and migratory. Both paradigms "explained" the plague, but appealed to different rules of authority (theory), thereby offering very different interpretations. Archaeologists too arrive at different explanations using the same set of objects. What is important to archaeology, however, is that "the explanation" be accurate and defendable, and further our knowledge about the past.

What often amounts to explanation in Egyptian archaeology is really description (see Chapter 5). Archaeologists must identify, describe, and catalog what they find, which results in long lists of objects, photographs of chosen pieces, and site drawings of where they were removed. Sometimes this may be an end in and of itself, but more often such descriptions are accompanied by additional speculations. This may be something as mundane as suggesting a type of lithic artifact carried out more than one task or how the inhabitants of a site fit into the surrounding community or into the national hierarchy. These are in effect attempts to explain the relationship between the artifacts and their human creators.

How do we judge the tenability of a particular explanation? That is, how do we decide if a hypothesis is a good fit to our collected data? If our hypothesis is a good one, our collected sample should be reasonably close to our expectations. If our collected sample provides a substantial deviation from our expectations, either our sample is inadequate or our hypothesis is incorrect. One way to assess a hypothesis is through a decision rule: a boundary formulated prior to the analysis or even collection of the data, which if exceeded violates the validity of the hypothesis. There is neither a rigid formula for determining what these boundaries are, nor a limit to the number of decision rules one can formulate for a given hypothesis. For this reason, archaeologists (as do most social scientists) fall back on accepted conventions.

The process of comparing viable hypotheses is usually called a test, and the competing hypotheses are framed within one or more boundaries.

For example, a hypothesis that explores our interest in Egyptian settlement patterns might be structured in the following way:

Ho: Egyptian settlement patterns were the same as those of Mesopotamia.

H1: Egyptian settlement patterns differed from Mesopotamia in that they depended on local geography and sociopolitical events.

From the archeological data, it seems that in many respects, Early Dynastic and Old Kingdom Egypt does present a contrast to contemporary Mesopotamia. Power and wealth for the latter were distributed among fortified urban city-states and among several competing interest groups within each urban center. These urban centers tended to be extremely large compared to other settlements, contained a diverse population from all socioeconomic levels, and interacted with the local populations through a market-based economy.

In contrast, Egypt seems to have maintained more of a rural character, with the population distributed among numerous small agricultural villages that interacted with the central authority in many unknown ways, but primarily, it is thought, through taxes and other appropriative measures.

From this brief summary we might infer that current information supports the H1 hypothesis, but how and in what way? In essence, the next set of questions is the more interesting:

Were Egyptian settlements sociopolitically organized into some hierarchical fashion?

Were they functionally dependent or interdependent?

Did population size and local geography play a significant role?

Looking at the problem from this more realistic perspective directs us away from the either/or structure of hypothesis testing to a more flexible method of evaluation using models.

A model, like a hypothesis, serves as a best-guess explanation for a group of artifacts. Whereas a hypothesis is often phrased in a cause-and-effect or either/or relationship, a model can be less restrictive and more flexible. A model seeks to represent phenomena, in our case artifacts and their associated past physical processes, in a logical and objective way. It is an attempt at creating a simplified view of the past for the purpose of better understanding certain aspects of the past.

As with a hypothesis, a model is evaluated first and foremost by its consistency with empirical data – the artifacts we retrieve. If a model is not consistent with our observations, it must be modified or rejected. Other factors important in evaluating a model include the ability to explain other instances of similar type or patterns of artifacts and its ability to predict future occurrences of similar artifacts and patterns. A model is not meant to be an absolute and accurate re-creation of the past, but rather a simplified perspective of certain aspects of the past constructed to enhance our understanding.

In creating and evaluating a model of how the Egyptian settlement system might have functioned, we want to use all available information. For example, epigraphic information has demonstrated that the ancient Egyptians recognized different types of settlements and used a number of terms to describe them. Unfortunately, the distinction between them is unclear. The most common term is *niwt,* (⊗̲) usually translated as "city" or "village," but in many cases it simply implies a community. The glyph, thought to represent a round settlement with intersecting streets (⊗), was used as a generic determinative for any community. *Niwt* could also denote a large city; for example, in the New Kingdom, Thebes, the theocratic center of the country and certainly one of the largest cities in Egypt, was referred to simply as *niwt,* "the city." The term *demy* (⌂𓀾𓏤), commonly translated as "town," may come from the root meaning "to touch," referring to an area of the riverbank where ships landed. Other words for types of settlements were *set* (𓊨), translated as "seat" or "abode," specifically that of a god; and *hwt* (𓉗), "domain," in reference to land holdings of a temple.

Useful though these terms may be, they provide few details of Egypt's ancient settlement system: the arrangement of communities in relation to each other in terms of their economy and social structure. For example, it is unclear whether and to what degree provincial settlements produced their own essential goods and services, interacting with the central authority only through taxes and tribute, or whether they were part of a larger regional production and exchange system with numerous connections. The fact that archaeologists have recovered large quantities of standardized pottery and other artifacts throughout the Nile Valley suggests a high degree of networking and a centralized authority. Investigations of Predynastic sites reveal a trend toward functional interdependence among some of the larger excavated settlements but the question remains whether this interdependence was true of smaller communities and carried over into the Old Kingdom, with its strong central government.

Old Kingdom Egypt can certainly be characterized as having a strong central government, along with an extensive system of taxation to support state projects and an administrative class to direct these works under the authority of the king. The working and peasant class, the bulk of the Egyptian population that supported the state apparatus, was to a great extent invisible, known only from tomb paintings and offering texts where they are portrayed conducting the activities required to support the tomb owner in the afterlife. This population, which was dispersed throughout the country in a variety of towns and villages, is little known archaeologically.

In concordance with textual evidence, Old Kingdom deposits have revealed several different types of settlements ranging from small rural villages to large population centers. Until recently, however, little work had been conducted on these sites to address questions related to their economic structure and sociopolitical position. In fact, only recently have scholars working in Egypt even thought about the most fundamental aspects of settlement archaeology: how to define different kinds of settlements. Logically, any investigation of Egyptian settlements must begin by first defining how one would classify a city, town, or village.

Although the problem seems a minor one, classifying settlement types is anything but straightforward when dealing with archaeological remains. For example, archaeologists have traditionally based their definition of a city on the ancient Mesopotamian form – that is, a walled community with continuous long-term habitation. Using this definition of "city" led to the earlier statement made by anthropologist John Wilson that Egypt was a civilization without cities. The Mesopotamian model, however, probably should not be applied to the Egyptian settlement pattern because the topography and society of the Nile Valley differed dramatically from that of ancient Iraq. Old Kingdom Egypt certainly had large population centers that would qualify as cities. In the later periods, for example, Memphis was composed of many neighborhoods and was spread out over many kilometers. According to classical writers, it took a full day to walk across the ruins. Nevertheless, it probably had no more than about 50,000 inhabitants, and most of them were devoted to the government. It was not the densely populated walled city one envisions when thinking of ancient city-states. What made it territorially large was that as it grew, it incorporated a number of villages, so there remained considerable space devoted to agriculture and other activities.

Because Egypt's frontiers were protected by vast deserts and seas, and the Nile offered equal access to goods and natural resources, there was no need to fortify cities behind walls. The greater population could live safely, dispersed across the valley. It is, therefore, probably incorrect to say that Egypt lacked cities: It simply did not have cities such as those in Mesopotamia. Making any definition operational, however, does pose its own set of problems. How does one differentiate between a city, town or village archaeologically? Although we can separate settlements into distinct entities, in reality they fall along a continuum, and how they are identified in the field remains difficult. With no generally accepted mechanisms in place, simple comparison and description remains the most common approach.

One basic way to establish a settlement hierarchy is by analyzing the number of functions carried out within a population center. That is, settlements can be differentiated archaeologically by noting what kinds of activities were conducted within each of the respective communities. Defined in this manner, a city is a multifunctional settlement that had a dominant regional position among other settlements that perform fewer functions. A town, on the other hand, served a number of different roles, ranging from market exchange to agriculture and government affairs, but differed from cities in that it maintained a strong agricultural component by offering attractive conveniences to agriculturally based communities (villages) located within easy traveling distance. Cities, although often maintaining an agricultural component, serve a greater variety of regional and national administrative functions than towns. In villages, only one or two functions, primarily agriculture, might be performed. In terms of population, which can loosely be interpreted archaeologically by the size of the settlement and number of structures, separating a city from a town might be difficult, but identifying a village with its limited functions and small population is more easily managed.

Questions regarding the type and size of Egyptian settlements and how they articulated with each other and with the central government are limited by the fact that what little work has been done has provided, at best, an unbalanced picture of the past. Although several large settlement sites have been excavated, and they have provided a wealth of information, the compiled research has yet to reach a point where we might comfortably classify them: Settlements still look unique because so few have been fully studied.

One of the ironies of Egyptian archaeology is that Egypt, from its inception to its final collapse, was dominated by village-sized agricultural communities, yet we know little archaeologically about villages and village life. Based on a number of regional surveys we do know that villages were numerous, that they tended to be located on levees adjacent to the river in Upper Egypt and on *geziras* (naturally occurring elevated mounds) near major tributaries in the Delta: Both locations offered the inhabitants safety from all but the highest of floods, and they did not take up cultivable lands (Figure 6.1). From our knowledge of Pre- and Early Dynastic settlements, we assume Old Kingdom villages to have been small, somewhat oval in plan, with mudbrick or thatch huts. The inhabitants, who were probably members of a single or several extended families, were primarily involved in agriculture. How independently they operated from other villages and larger, regionally dominant settlements remains unclear.

Research conducted at larger settlements have served to shed some light on the workings of nearby villages. Three important excavations have provided initial data to build an explanatory model for Egypt's sociopolitical workings at the regional level (Figure 6.2). Each of the three settlements provides a different look at the inner workings of the Old Kingdom state, and each

FIGURE 6.1. Modern villages, like ancient ones, are often situated atop delta *geziras*. The distant village rising above the lowlands is situated on an ancient *gezira* (photo by D. J. Brewer).

adds breadth to our overall understanding of settlement articulation with the central government.

GIZA

The social and economic history of the pyramids involved more than just the builders and their support network. Old Kingdom documents draw our attention to other institutions that existed near the pyramids long after the workers had left. From titles inscribed in tombs and from royal decrees we know that housing for priests and other functionaries must have been situated somewhere near the tombs. Other sources such as the Abu Sir Papyri also inform us of economic and social institutions that supported the functioning of the pyramid site as a center for ritual and these people, too, must have lived somewhere nearby.

To identify a likely site for a "pyramid community," archaeologist Mark Lehner and his team used "Holmesian logic" (i.e., purposive sampling): The ancient settlement had to lie a safe distance beyond the limestone quarry used to provide the core stones for the construction of the pyramid, and the settlement needed to be near an access route for the delivery of materials used

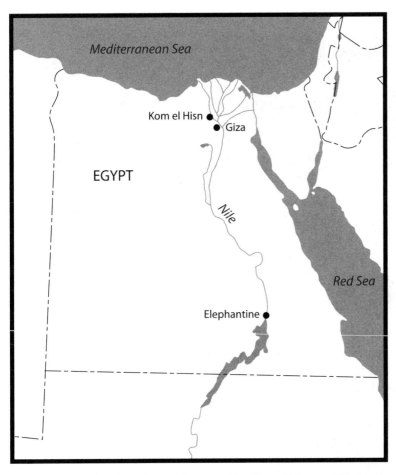

FIGURE 6.2. Location of the three settlements, Giza, Kom el-Hisn, and Elephantine, discussed in the text (Ault and Flores).

to supply the builders and outfitters of the tombs. They chose the mouth of a large wadi that they felt held the highest likelihood for settlement remains. They also chose to work in a second area west of the second pyramid, where tradition has it that the workmen were barracked. The archaeological materials recovered from this area soon showed the site to be a craft production and storage area, not a barracks, and so emphasis was shifted totally to the mouth of the wadi where a 5.4-hectare area was cleared of its sandy overburden, exposing the surface of an Old Kingdom settlement.

Over several seasons of work, nearly 500,000 pottery fragments were recovered from the excavations; 150,000 fragments were large enough and in good enough condition to be assigned to a type. Roughly 50 percent of the sherds

(a)   (b)

FIGURE 6.3. A typical carinated bowl (a) and a bread mold (b) recovered from Giza excavations (a: Courtesy of the Oriental Institute of the University of Chicago, b: © 2012 Museum Fine Arts Boston).

came from bread molds, followed by a crude redware jar. The third most abundant pottery type was a 20-centimeter-wide carinated bowl (Figure 6.3). Very few sherds from periods later than Dynasty 4 were recovered, and those that were appeared to be intrusive artifacts from later occupation. Excavations also produced 1,426 clay seals, of which 470 were impressed with text. Fifty of the legible fragments had royal names: Six belonged to Khafre and twelve to Menkaure. The remaining thirty-two inscribed sealings were less certainly translated, but three were thought to be from Khafra and twenty-nine from Menkaure. No other names of kings could be recognized.

The ceramic evidence and inscriptions suggest that the settlement was abandoned soon after Menkaure's rule. This would compare closely with historical sources, which indicate the royal funerary complex and its center of administration moved to Saqqara under Menkaure's successor, King Shepseskaf.

The horizontal plan of the excavations revealed four large quadrangles (approx. 34.5 × 52 meters) within which were long narrow subdivisions (approx. 5 × 35 meters), called "galleries" by the excavators. Each of the narrow galleries was divided down the middle by a bench made of small stones faced with mud and plaster (Figure 6.4a, b). This construction was apparently a support foundation for a series of wood columns spaced about 2.6 meters apart (i.e., 5 Egyptian cubits). In the front of one of these galleries, set just under the roof of the colonnade, was a nearly perfect circle of burnt earthen floor, one cubit in diameter, which was thought to be from an oven or hearth. At the opposite or south end of the galleries the space was partitioned into rooms that the excavators believed resembled living quarters, with a kitchen and sleeping areas.

GALLERY EXCAVATION PLAN

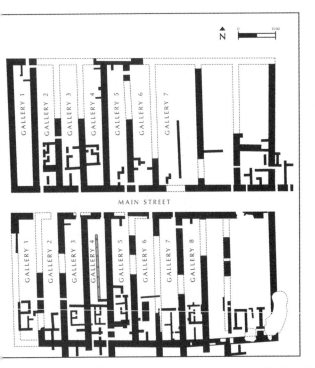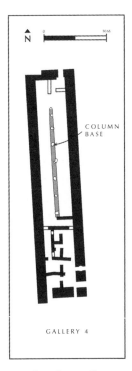

FIGURE 6.4. Horizontal plan of the Gallery Excavations (left) and a close-up plan of one gallery (right) (Jackie Gardner after Lehner 2002, figures 4 and 5).

Taken in its entirety, the excavations revealed a large complicated settlement crisscrossed with streets and lined by craft shops, bakeries, production areas, administrative buildings, and evidence of other diverse activities. The complex was well laid out as if by a predetermined plan – a very different configuration than what one expects from a "home-grown" settlement where ad hoc construction leads to complicated floor plans and twisting streets. The question that remained, however, was who lived in the town and why were they there?

Herodotus states that 100,000 men worked to build the pyramids over a period of twenty years. More recent estimates have placed this figure at somewhere around 25,000 people, which included not only masons and others who toiled on the structures, but also those who held support roles such as food preparers, toolmakers, and other craftsmen. The excavators were admittedly perplexed by the lack of ancient living debris such as broken pottery, ash, and animal bones that one would expect to be associated with such a large contingent of workers. They were also quite surprised to find such large empty spaces, principally the long colonnaded corridors in each of the gallery structures.

Practicing what is called "experimental archaeology," the team members themselves lay down in the galleries to see how many people the galleries might actually accommodate. Lying side by side, they estimated that one gallery could comfortably accommodate forty to fifty people. The entire gallery complex could then have sheltered as many as 1,600 to 2,000 people. Given the structure of the galleries, project director Mark Lehner hypothesizes that perhaps the gallery housed laborers in the more open areas in the north of the gallery and the overseer lived in the more elaborate quarters built at the south end of each gallery. The archaeologists could not determine what part of the labor force might have been quartered there.

They did believe, however, that if forty to fifty people were housed in each of the galleries, housing some two thousand people in all, this represented a well-organized workforce where close living and communal dining (perhaps the long, low bench served as "communal table") developed a strong esprit de corps. The large quantities of meat-bearing bones recovered from the site, including those of sheep, goat, and particularly cattle, further suggest that the building project was a large-scale fellowship or even a ritual event. The quantity and quality of red meat consumed was certainly more abundant and varied than a peasant or laborer could expect to enjoy living in his or her own home. Thus, working in honor of the king may have offered a number of benefits and perhaps some measure of status.

KOM EL-HISN

Unlike the pyramid settlement, Old Kingdom Kom el-Hisn was located far from the central authority of Egypt's ruling class. The site, at the western edge of the Delta, was situated near the extinct Canopic branch of the Nile (Figure 6.2). Radiocarbon dates, together with epigraphic finds and diagnostic artifacts such as pottery, place the settlement in the fifth and sixth Dynasties (ca. 2500–2290 BC), with sections of the site extending into the Middle and New Kingdom periods.

Modern research at Kom el-Hisn began in 1984, on the Old Kingdom occupation levels. Using a stratified random sampling design, the site was gridded and a series of 2 × 2–meter units were chosen for excavation. In addition, a 72-square-meter area was cleared of overburden to reveal architectural relationships, and two step trenches were excavated to reveal ancient topographic

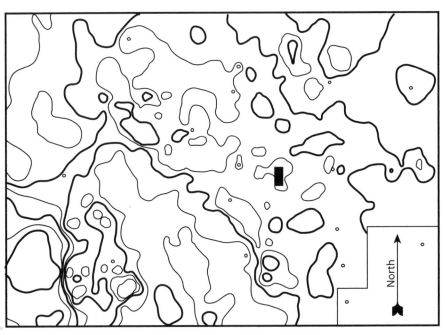

FIGURE 6.5. The archaeologists' topographic map of the Kom el-Hisn study area. Note the excavation unit (Figure 6.6) delineated in black (Ault and Flores after Wenke et al. 1988, figure 4).

features (Figure 6.5). The purpose of this stage of the project was to clarify the overall structure of the site as far as was possible (given time and budget) and to obtain a representative sample of ceramics and other artifacts.

Based on recovered artifacts, results show that the occupation area selected for excavation was indeed Old Kingdom in age. Most vessel forms were indicative of Dynasty 5–6 and known from other Old Kingdom occupations of similar age, primarily Giza and Saqqara. Architecture from the site is mostly domestic, with no use of stone. A large enclosure wall seems to surround at least a portion of the site. Excavation director Robert Wenke suspects that an administrative or religious sector was located in the southwestern portion of the site, but it is now almost entirely obscured by a modern village. The settlement itself (Figure 6.6) appears typical of the period, with a warren of enclosed spaces accessed by narrow winding streets or paths, with various functions being performed in different parts of the settlement. There appear to be two, possibly three, building episodes at the site. Rather than repair or build on to existing structures, it seems the inhabitants leveled the standing architecture, then backfilled the areas before commencing with new construction. Lithic artifacts included blades and sickle blades, the latter being well-worn, indicating extensive use in the harvesting of grains. The lack of extensive debitage and cores suggests that lithic production took place off-site. Animal remains indicate a mixed diet of sheep, goat, pigs, cattle (although rare), and wild game, most notably fish.

Paleobotanists noted that the distribution of four different classes of plant remains (cereal straw, field weeds, sedges, and fodder plants) differed from those at other Old Kingdom sites. Fodder plants (clover and vetch) comprised over one quarter of the analyzed remains, suggesting an important Kom el-Hisn industry was raising livestock. Because sheep and particularly goats have rather wide dietary ranges and do well browsing on available vegetation, the cultivation of clover and vetch suggests cattle rearing. Cattle have considerably higher water requirements than sheep and goats and require higher quality feed, particularly green grasses and other types of fresh plants, which have higher nutritional values than dry or dead forage. This supposition is further supported by the recovery of fodder plant remains in fire hearths, most likely the result of using dried dung as fuel. The fact that many of the ceramic types analyzed were similar to those of administrative and mortuary centers at Giza suggested to the archaeologists that perhaps Kom el-Hisn was providing cattle to other centers in exchange for necessities not produced in the community. Dedications to the cow goddess Hathor stimulated further speculation that a cult temple might have been located at Kom el-Hisn, underscoring its role as a producer of cattle for elite uses.

Two other important determinations were made through site excavations. The first was that the artifact classes (lithics, pottery, etc.) and their defined types were not randomly scattered across the site but tended to be focused in particular places, and certain types tended to co-occur. This was suggested as evidence of different activity areas across the site and for the presence of a two-tiered social system – an elite class and a peasant or worker class. This was most dramatically demonstrated through the analysis of faunal remains, where bones of sheep and goat predominated in what was thought to be the more elite areas of the site, and pig bones predominated in areas most likely occupied by peasants and laborers.

What the archaeologists were able to conclude about Kom el-Hisn was that in many ways, it depended on the surrounding area for some of its needs but in other ways, it was self-sufficient. There did not seem to be any evidence of craft production such as pottery or lithics at the site, so these would have had to be imported. Sheep, goat, and pigs were apparently raised and consumed on-site, and wild game supplemented the diet. Numerous sickle blades were

KOM EL-HISN

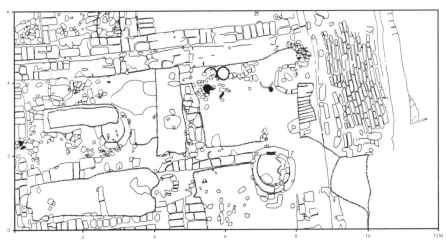

FIGURE 6.6. Horizontal excavation plan of the central area of the Kom el-Hisn excavations (Jackie Gardner after Wenke 1988 et al., figure 5).

found, many quite worn, which suggests local inhabitants were involved in harvesting grain; whether the fields were private, cult-, or government-owned is not certain. Considerable evidence for raising cattle existed but it seems few were consumed at the site, leading archaeologists to conclude that Kom el-Hisn was a cattle exporter and, in turn, imported other necessities.

Although it was situated in a remote area of the kingdom, Kom el-Hisn, rather than being isolated from state control, seemed closely connected to it via cattle production. Later texts in fact do corroborate that Kom el-Hisn supplied cattle to Egypt's cult centers. Nevertheless, Kom el-Hisn maintained a strong level of independence by producing its own food and engaging in commerce with the surrounding region.

ELEPHANTINE

Geography, probably more so than any other single factor, influenced settlement placement and population distribution at Elephantine (Figure 6.2). Situated at the southern border of Egypt, where an outcrop of basaltic rock created the first cataracts of the Nile, Elephantine holds a commanding position for the defense of the river – the main southern entry point into Egypt for goods and people. The settlement itself was placed on the southern tip of a large mid-channel island lying where the river, after passing through the rapids, resumes its tranquil course north.

The first cataract region was viewed as a boundary separating Egyptian and Nubian spheres of influence. Not strictly a border, the area is probably best viewed as a broad transitional zone with a mixing of cultural materials. For example, it is not unusual to find Nubian A-Group pottery fragments in Predynastic sediments near Elephantine, although they become increasingly rare just a little further downstream. Naturally, this border area was an important trade zone between Nubia and Egypt dating back to at least the late Predynastic.

In contrast to other important provincial towns where abundant agricultural land was a common feature, Elephantine's land situation is rather extreme, imposing limits on settlement size and distribution. Although blessed by its strategic position, the Elephantine area lacked the farmlands needed to support a large population. In general, farmland was limited to a narrow strip along the riverbanks, restricting early villages to embayments and wadi mouths. By far the largest expanse of available cultivable land was in the wide embayment on the east bank of the Nile that today is occupied by the modern town of Aswan.

The local Predynastic population adjusting to the paucity of agricultural lands adopted a dispersed settlement pattern. The distribution of Predynastic cemeteries suggests that villages were strung out along the river's edge at 6-kilometer intervals, far enough apart that a sustained livelihood could be maintained throughout the region. This pattern dramatically changed at the beginning of the Dynastic period.

Although lacking in cultivable lands, Elephantine did possess two important resources that contributed to its long-term success. The most obvious was its location, straddling the main trade route between Egypt and sub-Saharan Africa. The second important trait was its geological richness, specifically granite and crystalline rocks. The granite was valued for monumental architecture and the crystalline stone for creating stone vessels and jewelry.

The original settlement of Elephantine dates to Naqada II, but the area may have been occupied earlier. That this was the ancestor to the later Dynastic settlement is supported by the discovery of a Dynasty 1 temple dedicated to Satet, goddess and mistress of Elephantine, whose cult can be followed archaeologically in an unbroken sequence to Ptolemaic times.

No doubt a turning point for the settlement occurred in Dynasty 1, when a fort was constructed. Unfortunately, most of the fort is now covered by modern construction – the new antiquities museum. What can be determined is that the fort was protected by double walls originally built in straight lines over uneven ground, standing about 3 meters high. The outer wall, approximately

50 × 50 meters, was strengthened by transecting inner walls and by the placement of semicircular (and one rectangular) watchtowers at each of the corners. The fortification was situated on an elevated part of the island where it overlooked the best quay. Clearly this position was strategically chosen to extend control over the river and its use as a highway for the transportation of goods into and out of Egypt. Only a small part of the interior of the fortress could be excavated, and the domestic architecture here appeared no different from the huts found in the village outside the fort.

In exploring the relationship between the fortress and the settlement (Figure 6.7), the excavator Martin Ziermann believes that the planning and construction of the fort bears witness to considerable know-how not previously attested to at the site. The fortress site was situated in the optimal position for controlling river traffic; the builders, it seems, were not concerned with the settlement but rather with what the site's geography offered over the river. The power of the central authority was unequivocally expressed when the archaeologists discovered that the fortress crosscut the front of a pre-existing temple, eliminating much of its forecourt and forcing the local inhabitants to relocate its entrance to another part of the structure. This strongly implies that the fort's construction was directed from outside the region and that its construction superseded local authority. More than just a bureaucratic checkpoint, the fort also appears to have been built to extend Egypt's power over Nubia and to circumvent Nubia's role as a middleman in trade with the African cultures farther to the south. This mission seems to have been accomplished as the A-Group economy and culture seems to have quickly dissolved and disappeared, at least archaeologically, from the area. Nubian culture does make a comeback, however, when Egypt's central authority became weak or nonexistent.

Apparently, at Elephantine, the early Egyptian state used its authority to establish state institutions, thereby changing the sociopolitical makeup of the area in innumerable ways. One way to detect these changes archaeologically is through studying the changing settlement patterns.

At Elephantine the introduction of central authority created a sociopolitical environment whereby villages once spaced at 6-kilometer intervals along the Nile suddenly disappeared. This phenomenon has been noted at several other areas in Egypt at about the same time. At Abydos and Hierakonpolis, villages scattered across the cultivable landscape were abandoned in favor of a single large town in which the regional population came to be concentrated. Such a pattern would have facilitated greater control over the populace by state authorities. Interestingly, in the First Intermediate Period and

Middle Kingdom, a time of reduced central control, the Predynastic settlement pattern (6-kilometer spacing) reasserts itself at Elephantine. Although the intrusion of the central government appears to have been unsympathetic to local cult temples, it does seem that the community benefited from the government's presence. The settlement was successful enough that it evolved into a fortified town that took on regional political importance, thereby gaining importance as a center for local trade and influence.

MODEL BUILDING

To summarize available evidence, many factors influenced the location of Egyptian settlements, such as geography, local economic pressures, and by Old Kingdom times, the central government. Synthesizeing the information from our admittedly small sample of three midsized settlements and how they functioned within the Old Kingdom state, it appears that although each has its own geographical setting and particular evolutionary history, all held specific connections to the central authority. Using our function-based definition, Elephantine and Kom el-Hisn were multifunctional communities and centers of trade. Each was part of an exchange network tapping local agriculturally based settlements (villages) for vital necessities, and was articulated with the central government through taxes and the exportation of locally abundant resources. In the case of Kom el-Hisn, the settlement appears to have supplied much of its own food but served the government by supplying cattle to the administration and its distributive networks in exchange for manufactured crafts such as pottery. Elephantine, with its prime geographic position, served as a border-town garrison, but its lack of agricultural land made it dependent on regional trade and probably government support to ensure its livelihood. This seems clear by the to-and-fro shift in the 6-kilometer spacing of settlements. Although Elephantine did provide exportable products in the form of granite and semiprecious stones, its location was the prime reason for investment by the central government.

The pyramid settlement poses an interesting case: Its very existence was a creation of the state. Planned communities such as the pyramid settlement seem to be more carefully laid out, with straighter streets and more uniform buildings in comparison to indigenously grown communities. The population and diversity of functions carried out at the site would suggest it was a town, but one of very limited scope. It is probably best to view it as an ancient version of a company town where its very existence was dependent on production, in this case the nearby pyramids. Like a company town, when the factory shuts

HORIZONTAL PLAN OF ELEPHANTINE

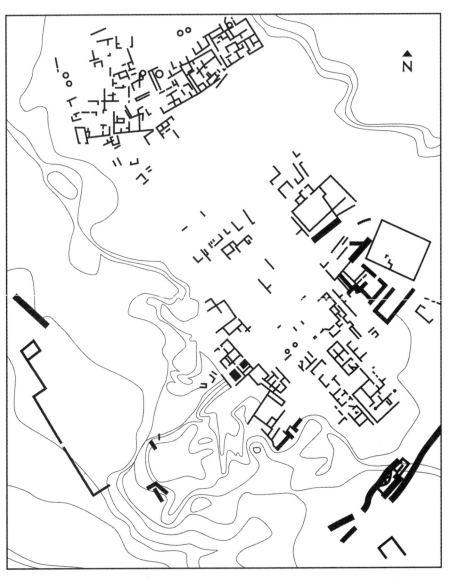

FIGURE 6.7. Horizontal plan of Elephantine (Jackie Gardner after Raue et al. 2004, figure 2).

down, so does the community, so when the government shifted operations to a new site, the pyramid town fell into disuse.

What large towns such as Kom el-Hisn and Elephantine had in common was that they served as centers for meeting local as well as national needs in terms of trade, taxes, and communication. It is more likely than not that because of their size and regional influence that in time they carried out some state bureaucratic functions, even to the point of being the regional nome capital in the case of Elephantine. Small villages surrounding the towns, we would predict, would depend on these centers for many types of goods not locally produced. Taxes too would have been a subject of interaction between villages and a regional center. An agriculture-based village, we presume, would have been levied appropriate taxes collected by officials in the regional center, with any surplus production bartered for pottery, tools, and other needed commodities.

If this were the case, a single large population center would accommodate the needs of many small villages. A city would have served a number of towns and associated villages. In fact, it would need the food produced at these villages to support its population, many of whom would be involved in non-agricultural activities. As well, the government would need some mechanisms for controlling incoming and outgoing tax revenues. Site visits to every village farm plot would have been impractical for royal authorities, but not for a local civil service, which probably worked out of the dominant town in the region and reported to the nome capital or the capital city. If this model were correct, we would expect to find a group of villages geographically situated around a larger population center, the larger center in turn serving a bureaucratic function between state and hinterland.

EVALUATING THE MODEL: PREDICTING SETTLEMENT PATTERNS

When working at Mendes, a large site in the east central Delta, we also explored the regional interconnections. The problem we faced was that the entire area was under cultivation or inhabited, rendering the traditional foot survey impractical. We decided to employ SPOT satellite imagery (Satellite Pour l'Observation de la Terre) to locate potential sites and then validate the finds through on-ground inspection of the computer-generated locales (Figure 6.8). The computer-enhanced satellite image was directed to look for reflective light properties of Old Kingdom mudbrick architecture; in so doing, we identified forty-one sites ranging from Neolithic to Roman in age. Fully one-half (probably more) were shown to have an Old Kingdom component. In addition, we identified seven sites that the satellite missed because they lacked mudbrick architecture.

FIGURE 6.8. SPOT Satellite image of delta showing Predynastic sites. The dark rectangular areas near the center of the image represent ancient mudbrick walls (photo of D. J. Brewer).

From this analysis, we suggest that the ancient town of Mendes appears to have served as a center for many smaller village-sized communities (Figure 6.9). A Dutch survey in the east central Delta found a similar pattern, locating fourteen small Old Kingdom settlements (villages?) in a 10 × 20 kilometer area, as well as a number of large tells thought to be the remains of larger population centers perhaps serving the role of a regional town.

Our model, in which large Egyptian population centers served as focal points for local trade and interregional commerce as well as points of articulation with the central government, seems to be supported by the Delta survey data as well as the information from the Elephantine, Kom el-Hisn, and Giza excavations. Villages seemed to have helped support the government via taxes and towns by supplying needed foodstuffs. In exchange, they bartered surplus agricultural products for needed manufactured goods. Although making our definitions operational archaeologically has left us with some gaps in the relationships between towns and cities, textual data has provided important documentation of such interactions. Surveying textural sources, geographer

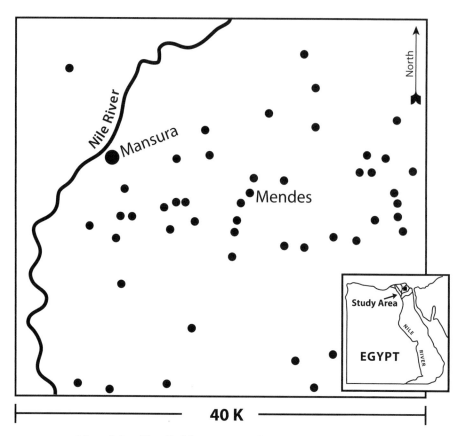

FIGURE 6.9. Map of sites identified by SPOT Satellite and corroborated by archaeological survey (by Ault and Flores).

and environmental archaeologist Karl Butzer identified 18 settlements that could be classified as cities, 27 as large towns, thirty-three as small towns, and 139 as large villages. Hamlet and small village-sized communities were not represented in the documents, probably because ancient tax roles and ideology focused on the larger settlements. Nevertheless, the distribution of cities to large and small communities falls well within our developing model.

Egypt, it seems, was highly urbanized, and there was an array of settlement types ranging from cities to towns to small villages. Each was incorporated into a working bureaucratic network through taxation, corvée labor, and at local levels, the exchange of goods. Interdependency rather than self-sufficiency seems to be the pattern in Egypt, and although the appearance of Egyptian cities differs from those of Mesopotamia, an equally elaborate network of communities and functions existed and interacted with the central government.

Naturally our model is just a starting point and needs to be further evaluated by additional examples and data collected from other areas of Egypt. This may lead to adjustments in our model or the rise of a completely new interpretative model to explain the Egyptian settlement system and its articulation with the state.

7

STABILITY AND PROVINCIALISM: ARCHAEOLOGY AND THE ENVIRONMENT

The ancient Egyptians interacted with their environment in many ways, and in turn the environment left its imprint on Egyptian culture (Figure 7.1). Viewing Egypt's past through its relationship with the environment falls under the collective subdiscipline of environmental archaeology, an umbrella term that encompasses biological and geological studies of the archaeological past.

Environmental archaeology is the study of the interaction between humans and their environment, with one of its common goals being to reconstruct the past environment of the site or region under study. It has emerged as a named discipline only in the last thirty years, but in that time has become one of the most popular approaches to archaeological interpretations of the past. Its significance can be attested to in its growth as a major component to most excavation projects, which now often include specialists in geoarchaeology, archaeobotany, and zooarchaeology.

Environmental archaeology offers a particular challenge to its practitioners because they study and evaluate objects of the natural world, yet must apply it to explanations couched within a humanistic paradigm, all the while being cognizant of earlier archaeologists and their mistaken belief that the environment was the dominant or "the sole" factor in Egypt's social evolution, a view known as environmental determinism. In its strictest sense, environmental determinism holds that the environment directly determines human behavior and society, a position not looked upon with much favor in our more enlightened times.

Unfortunately, environmental determinism, although offering some thought-provoking points, has left a scar on archaeology, with many scholars reacting negatively to any suggestion that the environment shapes human society. Nevertheless, it is hard to deny that many aspects of Egyptian culture were anything but environmentally related. The rhythm of the Nile influenced what crops to plant and when, the placement of settlements, the creation of

(a)

(b)

(c)

FIGURE 7.1. Natural motifs in day-to-day Egyptian objects: (a) hieroglyphs, (b) papyrus columns, (c) temple pylon entrance (a: Erich Lessing/Art Resource, NY, Oriental Institute of the University of Chicago; b: © DeA Picture Library/Art Resource, NY; c: photo by D. Brewer).

FIGURE 7.2. The Nile inundation (ca. AD 1900) before the construction of the Aswan Dam (photography collection, Miriam and Ira D. Wallach Division of Art, Prints and Photographs, The New York Public Library, Astor, Lenox and Tilden Foundations).

certain technologies such as water management, and modes of river travel; even metaphysical beliefs related back to the environment. It is little wonder then that changes in Egypt's riverine environment had profound effects on the population: Exceptionally low or high floods could wreak havoc across the countryside and lead to disastrous crop failures (Figure 7.2). The key difference between these correlations and old-style environmental determinism is that the environment is seen as contributing to culture change rather than determining the outcome, a subtle but important point.

Probably one of the earliest examples of an explanation couched within environmental archaeology is the now-famous Oasis Hypothesis, which attempted to explain the origins of agriculture in terms of the climatic changes associated with the end of the Pleistocene some 10,000 years ago. Various scholars suggest that the world became warmer and drier at this time, and people, animals, and plants were then forced into close proximity, out of which arose domestication. The Oasis Hypothesis was accepted in whole or in part for decades. One need only think of Egypt's Fayum and the early evidence for domestication found there as an example of the hypothesis's potential validity. Eventually, however, it was demonstrated that the wild ancestors of wheat and barley did not grow in the areas where people were thought to have been concentrated, and there was additional evidence that the deserts and oases of today were not formed in Asia and North Africa at the time of domestication. Nevertheless, even though the Oasis Hypothesis has been discarded, modern attempts to explain cultural change in Egypt often still rely on environmental change, and incorporating environmental data into Egyptian archaeology has become routine.

GEOARCHAEOLOGY, ARCHAEOBOTANY, AND ZOOARCHAEOLOGY

From the beginning, the goal of environmental archaeology has been the inter-disciplinary analysis of the geographical environment inhabited by ancient populations. Practitioners in the field fall in two general disciplinary groups. The first one, geoarchaeology, concentrates predominantly on the natural geographical context of archaeological objects. Its practitioners use geology, geomorphology, and climatology in order to reconstruct the circumstances that influenced the location of archaeological sites, the formation of cultural remains, and their depositional history. The second group, which includes archaeobotanists and zooarchaeologists, concentrates its attention on the eco-logical links between human society and the natural environment. Originally, environmental analyses were carried out by biologists and geologists, but now are almost exclusively done by archaeologists trained in the geological or biological sciences.

We have dealt with geology's contributions to archaeology in previous chapters, most notably in our discussion of the Paleolithic. As with geol-ogy, geoarchaeology is a broad field of inquiry. Geoarchaeologists working in Egypt, like elsewhere in the world, generally focus on the sedimentary processes associated with site formation and regional geological processes (see Figs. 2.1 and 3.4). However, they also study aeolian formations such as sand dunes and their movements, fluvial transport of sediments, soil analysis, and the geomorphology of the river through time, just to name a few of their research endeavors.

Archaeobotany is concerned with the study of plant remains, mainly macro-remains such as seeds and wood but also micro-remains such as pollen, preserved in association with archaeological sites (Figure 7.3). Archaeobotany is interested in all activities carried out by past populations, but the most

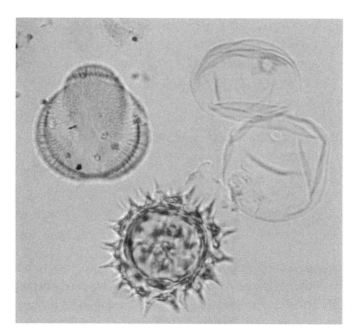

FIGURE 7.3. Archaeologically recovered pollen sample of a typical arid environment with Artemisia (upper left), grass (upper right), and a composite (courtesy of James C. Chatters).

predominant is subsistence: what food people ate, how they obtained it, and how and where they stored and processed it. Archaeobotanists also look at trade, construction materials, and aspects of ritual. In addition, archaeobotany provides information about past environments.

Zooarchaeology is the study of faunal remains associated with archaeological sites. Zooarchaeologists examine skeletal remains, mollusk shells, and insect parts for the purpose of better understanding past diets, procurement strategies (i.e., hunting and fishing practices), and the environment within which these activities occurred (Figure 7.4).

The use of floral and faunal remains to assess past environments is at one level relatively straightforward. The recovery of fish bones, a common element of Nile Valley sites, serves as an example (although one could use seeds or pollen). The skeletal elements, once identified, can offer information not only on ancient diets but also the past environment because of the creatures' habitat preferences. Adult Nile perch, for example, prefer to inhabit deep, well-oxygenated waters. Nile catfish, on the other hand, prefer swampy, deoxygenated waters. This information, combined with data from other recovered species, can offer clues as to what the ancient environment around the site looked like when these taxa were harvested as well as what

FIGURE 7.4. Faunal remains embedded in ancient lakeshore mud (photo by D. J. Brewer).

technologies were used to capture the fish. Simply put, if a plant or animal is identified from archaeological contexts, it is assumed that those requirements necessary for its survival existed somewhere in the area.

If archaeological inferences are based on a conservative presence/absence of taxa as in the preceding example, then few complicated assumptions are necessary to support a conclusion. Problems arise, however when attempts are made to use the data at higher levels of inference. For example, what does it mean when 300 Nile perch, 150 catfish, 6 gazelle, and 3 goat bones are recovered? Remaining conservative and using only a nominal (presence/absence) level of measurement (Table 7.1), one could postulate the existence of deep and shallow waters and open wadis with some browsing vegetation, but how does one decide which environment was dominant, or which taxa were more important to the diet?

Questions such as these require the use of different scales of measurement (ordinal and ratio), which in turn requires a number of assumptions to be made by the analyst. Accepting that the number of identified bones of a species represents the number of animals originally deposited at the site (a ratio level measurement) assumes that all species have the same number of identifiable bones, and that each skeletal element survives the ravages of time equally – assumptions that simply are not true. One can never be sure that 300 bones of species A represents two times more animals than 150 bones of species B.

TABLE 7.1. *Levels of measurement and associated assumptions*

Presence/Absence:	an item or class is simply present or absent such that item A is present or it is not present. No other assumptions of measurement are made or inferred.
Ordinal:	an item or class can be said to be more or less abundant than another, but how much more or less abundant cannot be ascertained, such that A is more abundant that B and B is greater than C. There is no valid figure for determining how much more abundant A is to B or C, only that one is more abundant that the other.
Ratio:	measured distances between items or classes truthfully represent the actual variable of distance between the items/classes measured, such that if A is 10 and B is 5, A is truly twice as abundant as B.
Interval:	as in a ratio scale except the value of 0 is arbitrary, as in 0°C. The value 0 does not mean there is no temperature but refers to a value labeled 0. (A ratio level value of 0 means that no item or value exists, such as 0 kilograms or 0 potsherds.)

In fact, it might not even represent two times as many animals if both A and B were the same species. Volumes of literature have been written on how to make valid cross comparisons, but all formulas remain controversial. Nevertheless, looking at the same set of data at the ordinal level, one might be able to say with some statistical assurances that species A was more numerous than species B, but how much more numerous may not be known.

Archaeologists must (although many do not) consider the nature of their data and choose a level of measurement commensurate with the limits of the data they employ. Given the unknown nature of post-depositional processes on the skeletons of animals (called taphonomic processes), faunal analysts have determined that a ratio level of measurement may be an invalid one when working with archaeologically derived skeletal remains. We simply do not know what 300 Nile perch bones means, culturally or environmentally speaking. We can be certain that the fish bones were recovered and utilized (presence/absence data). We can also feel confident at times that 300 Nile perch bones demonstrates greater incidence in the environment or cultural usage than 25 catfish bones (ordinal measurement), but we can never be sure that 300 bones represents 12 times as many fish as 25 bones (ratio measurement).

Another way archaeologists derive environmental information from plant and skeletal remains is to study the specimens themselves. Using the Predynastic period as an example, it has been suggested (based on study of Nile perch vertebrae recovered from Hierakonpolis) that the environment at this critical

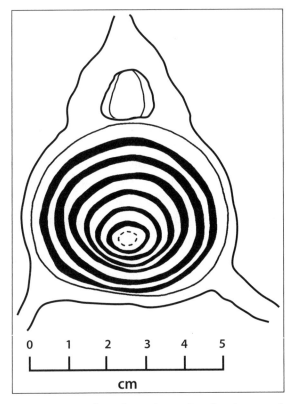

FIGURE 7.5. Schematic diagram of a Nile perch vertebra showing growth rings (Ault and Flores).

time became more variable when compared to today. Nile perch vertebrae, like those of many ectothermic (cold-blooded) animals, display a series of growth rings similar to those found on trees (Figure 7.5). Each year the perch lays down a ring that varies in width and bone density based on the water temperature – a narrow dark ring corresponding to cooler winter temperatures, and a wider, lighter-colored ring corresponding to warmer summer months and the growth period. Because ring width (and fish growth) depends in part on water temperatures, it provides a rough thermometer of the period in which the fish lived. Also, in Egypt there is a correlation between temperature and rainfall. The measured vertebrae indicate considerably more variation in temperature, and we thus can infer more variable rainfall during the Predynastic period than we see today. The geologist Judith Bunbury has also noted sediments indicative of very active wadis at Hierakonpolis during Predynastic times, suggesting large intermittent rainfalls. This in turn might account for the population movements away from the wadis and other changes noted archaeologically at Hierakonpolis during this time.

EGYPTIANS AND THEIR ENVIRONMENT

That Egyptians were aware of oscillations in their environment seems clear by their use of Nilometers to gauge the size of the Nile flood. Each year, summer monsoon rains in Ethiopia sent water cascading down the Blue Nile. In June this influx of floodwater could be detected in Aswan, and by mid-August in the Delta. The river would remain at flood height for forty to sixty days and then begin to recede. This annual phenomenon was responsible for Egypt's fertility, because with the floodwaters came 110 million tons of sediment washed down from the Ethiopian highlands. The floodwater irrigated the land and the sediment enriched the soil, but the floods were subject to variation. Floods that were as little as 50 centimeters lower than ideal would not extend to all the cultivable fields, and harvests would suffer, whereas floods that were 50 centimeters higher than ideal would remain too long on the fields and shorten the growing season. Additionally, unusually high floods might damage dikes and even threaten villages.

Nilometers were positioned along the river, and the measurements were calibrated to predict poor, good, and excessive flood heights. Although current evidence does not indicate that the Egyptians transformed the Nilometer readings into useful measures for predicting crop yields, they most certainly understood the implications of a normal, low, or high flood and prepared accordingly.

Harold Hurst's 1952 publication is among the most comprehensive study of Nile floods to date. He based his work on historically recorded Nilometer readings (AD 622–1522) and twentieth-century records of Nile water discharge. Both data sets resulted in normal distribution curves, indicating that high floods were as common as low floods during both the twentieth century and historic times.

Hurst also demonstrated the existence of certain multi-decadal periods dominated by higher or lower than average floods. For example, particularly high flood levels were recorded from AD 1869 to 1898, whereas from AD 1899 to 1942 floods were particularly low. Yet even within these groupings, considerable variation existed. During the period of low floods (1899–1942), ten were considered high and two dangerously high. In addition, flood heights did not appear to be predictive of the following year's floods: During the period of recorded high floods (1869–98), the highest and lowest floods occurred in successive years, with a difference of 2.75 meters in peak height. All attempts by Hurst to define cyclical or modal patterning of flood heights failed.

In recognizing that the environment played a role in Egyptian history, comparing these natural oscillations to the historic record can result in interesting correlations that offer insights into understanding Egypt's past. Among the most tumultuous of periods in Egyptian history was the First Intermediate Period: a time of great civil strife followed by a period of calm prosperity, the Middle Kingdom. How and why Egypt fell into this "dark age" is still debated, but as research continues, an environmental element seems more and more probable.

THE FIRST INTERMEDIATE PERIOD

In the later dynasties of the Old Kingdom in the years leading up to the First Intermediate Period, the population of Egypt burgeoned, and so did the bureaucracy. To pay for the increased rolls of officials, the king assigned tracts of land to cover their wages. Also, overly pious kings continued to grant lands and tax-free status to temple estates. Over time, this policy served to diminish the royal treasuries. Although the prosperity of the country was more widely distributed across the population, less of it was in the hands of the central government, eventually leading to an impoverished monarchy no longer able to support the infrastructure of the government.

The redistribution of wealth also emboldened provincial rulers, who with their growing prosperity began managing the nomes as their own small kingdoms, eventually passing the position by heredity rather than royal appointment. A number of kings attempted to bring the nomarchs under greater central control, but to little avail. Pepi II, fourth and some say last king of Dynasty 6, appears to have made such moves, but at his death the nomarchs further empowered themselves by taking control of the temples located in their provinces and becoming their chief priests, thereby enhancing their authority and wealth and disregarding all but in name the primacy of the king.

It has always been considered a strong possibility that an environmental collapse might have been a contributing factor in the Old Kingdom's demise. There is textual and some pictorial evidence suggesting crop failures and food shortages at this time, and if crops did fail, the weakened government of the late Old Kingdom might not have been able to overcome the civil unrest ignited by mass food shortages.

How might the evidence for climatic change noted by textual sources be supported or refuted through archaeological analysis? Unfortunately, Egypt's First Intermediate Period culture is not well known, specifically because our traditional sources of information – statues, texts, and large elaborate tombs – are not abundant for this period. There are, nevertheless, a number of cemeteries dating to the First Intermediate Period that provide a view of the culture, and recent work on the ancient environment provides additional evidence.

THE CULTURAL EVIDENCE

Because death is almost always an emotional experience, much can be gleaned about a culture from the way it prepares its members for burial, and no culture went to greater extent in such preparations than the ancient Egyptians. Naturally it is the royal tombs, the richest and most spectacular, that grab public attention, but it is the average burial, the most representative of the general population, that provides information concerning the vast majority of the populace and its culture.

Often a physical anthropologist (osteologist) is a part of the excavation team and has the duties of removing and analyzing the skeletal remains. Once analyzed, the bones can provide details as to gender and age of the individual, what ailments afflicted him or her in life, and with chemical tests, what types of food were predominant in the diet (e.g., grains, meat, fish): An important avenue of research for corroborating floral and faunal studies. Data from a cemetery can provide demographic information as to average life expectancies, birth and death rates, and even some rough estimates as to the local village population size.

For example, studies on the skeletal remains recovered from First Intermediate Period and Middle Kingdom burials at Gebelein and Asyut provided some interesting insights into Egyptian life. Once in the lab, the skeletal remains were separated on the basis of gender. This was done based on measurements of the pelvis and the skull – females having a proportionally wider pelvis and males a number of more robust features on the skull. By studying the skull sutures and the degree of epiphysical fusion of the long bones, age estimates of the deceased were made.

Osteologists determined that for the interred population, the average age at death for males was estimated to be about thirty-six. Average age of death for females was thirty, although once a female reached thirty, there seemed to be a sharp decline in death rate, and life expectancy seemed to be equal to or exceed that of males. The high number of young female deaths correlates with their most productive child-bearing years: The stresses associated with pregnancy and giving birth under less-than-sanitary conditions clearly took a toll. A related fact derived from the skeletal study is that physically, these Egyptians appear to be a rather gracile population. Males averaged 157 centimeters in height, females 148 centimers, and both were characterized by curiously narrow pelvic girdles, a factor that certainly contributed to higher female mortality rates in childbirth.

Studies also showed this population suffered from iron deficiencies. The skulls showed a number of porosities associated with anemia. This could reflect an insufficient amount of iron entering the body or extensive affliction with diarrheal diseases, causing chronic blood loss. Endemic diseases such as schistosomiasis also can contribute to such a condition. Not surprisingly, this condition seems to be less predominant in burials of more elite individuals.

Tooth wear analysis showed that Egyptians display considerably more tooth wear than do modern populations and burials ascribed to upper classes showed less tooth wear than lower class individuals. Extensive tooth wear was attributed to foods eaten, as well as to the dirt, grit, and sand impurities in the food, particularly the flour used for bread. One additional practice that added significantly to tooth wear was the habit of chewing vegetable masticates, in particular papyrus, which requires strong pressures to break down its fibers, resulting in excessive tooth wear.

Gurob provided another example of a First Intermediate Period population. Many of the graves were no more than shallow holes with the deceased placed with the head to the north. Others were placed, lying on their left side, in simple wooden coffins. There were amazingly few grave goods. Many burials lacked even a single pottery vessel, and a single pot was the only grave good in other tombs. Graves with as many as three vessels were exceptional. Nevertheless, in a woman's grave a mirror was found, and in a man's tomb a copper adze (certainly a valuable object). A third tomb of a male contained a partly plastered coffin, one ceramic vessel, a string of beads with a silver pendant, and a copper dagger, which is thought to be a status symbol. An exceptional find in another burial is a small silver pendant in the form of two facing lions. The pendant is unusual in design and suggests its owner was a woman of wealth. As with the dagger and adze, burial goods seem to be objects used in daily life, not specifically made for burial.

The Qau-Mostagedda cemetery (Middle Egypt) offers another First Intermediate Period example. There, about 5,000 burials have been excavated ranging in age from Old Kingdom to Middle Kingdom. In general, the First Intermediate Period burials included the same range of objects as those found in Gurob but their overall richness far exceeds Gurob and other period cemeteries. This has elicited considerable discussion because it departs from the conventional picture of the First Intermediate Period as a time of political unrest and famine. Amulets such as small gold bird figurines, carnelian legs and hands, and button seals are typical finds, most probably elements from larger items of jewelry such as necklaces and armlets. Button seals (which metamorphosed into scarabs at the end of this period) were often found associated with women. Interestingly the later scarabs were worn by men. This suggests, but does not explain, a shift in function of these objects from jewelry to religious and status symbols used in the administration of royal or private estates for sealing goods and letters. The high frequency of gold and other quality goods suggests this region was wealthier than other areas.

In those First Intermediate Period tombs that contained coffins, regional differences could be identified when preservation was good enough for coffin texts and decorations to be preserved. In fact, it is very easy to distinguish cemeteries by their coffin style. For example at Akhmim (end of Sixth to Twelfth dynasties), offering lists are found on the outside of the coffin next to the wadjet eyes. Coffins recovered from Gebelein possess unique forms of hieroglyphs, and at Asyut, near the end of the First Intermediate Period, the lines of text found on the outside of the coffin are doubled. Interestingly, at Saqqara, the traditions of the Old Kingdom remained strong throughout the First Intermediate Period, so much so that it can be very difficult to distinguish between late Old Kingdom and First Intermediate Period coffins (Figure 7.6).

In general, excavated cemeteries of the First Intermediate Period give the impression that there were regional differences as to the severity of the times; provincial nobles seemed wealthier than their Old Kingdom counterparts, and to some degree larger sections of the general populace seemed to reflect greater wealth as well. The fragmentation of central government at the end of Dynasty 6 and the rise of local polities also led to differences in cultural expression that can be readily viewed in the regional cemeteries, particularly in the well-to-do graves.

By the end of the 12th Dynasty, the Egyptian state apparatus had not only fully recovered from the disunity of the First Intermediate Period but the country had fully matured into a vibrant, expanding culture. A classical period

(a)

(b)

FIGURE 7.6. Examples of First Intermediate Period coffins: (a) Dynasty 11, (b) Late Dynasty 11 or Early Dynasty 12 (a: © Virginia Museum of Fine Arts, Richmond. Adolph D. and Wilkins C. Williams Fund; b: photo by D. J. Brewer).

of literature had ensued. Craftsmanship, particularly in fine jewelry, reached a pinnacle in quality and style that was never surpassed. Up and down the Nile Valley, cities were governed by appointed mayors and assisted by a corps of lesser officials. Egypt controlled Nubia at least to the second cataract, and monitored the desert frontiers with sentinel posts and fortified barriers.

Similarly for the First Intermediate Period, the bulk of our archaeological information for the Middle Kingdom comes from provincial cemeteries, which bespeak a multitier social class system with a middle class made of minor officials, professional craftsmen, and prosperous civil servants. Burial customs did not change much between the First Intermediate Period and the Middle Kingdom. In fact, some tombs currently dated to the First Intermediate Period may belong to the early Middle Kingdom.

At the provincial level, the tombs and furnishings of the local ruling classes (Meir, Asyut, Beni Hasan) seem to be quite uniform and contain a high proportion of objects made especially for the tomb. Tombs are decorated and often contain decorated coffins and wood models of craftsmen working in shops and preparing food. The dead are often wrapped in linen but not often mummified. When the tombs are examined in detail, however, differences between regions still can be detected. Coffins from Middle Egypt (Asyut), for example, are adorned with double lines of inscriptions, whereas those found in Upper Egypt (Gebelein, Edfu) are decorated on the outside with scenes of daily life. These styles extending back into the First Intermediate Period suggest a lingering sense of regional identity and independence. Tomb decorations also exhibit regional differences. When comparing Beni Hassan with Meir coffins, one can see differences in quality and style of the artistic renderings.

Burials of the common peoples differ from those of officials in that the coffins are generally undecorated, and the deceased are not buried with objects made specifically for the tomb. Pottery for the eternal food supply, however, is ever-present. Women are often accompanied with jewelry that probably belonged to them in life; it is often well made and expensive. Tombs never seem to contain objects related to the owner's profession, and without tomb or coffin inscriptions, it is hard to know their place in life. Inscriptions seem restricted to elite burials, leaving tombs only divisible into rich or poor.

In sum, although much of what we know about the First Intermediate Period and Middle Kingdom comes from texts, archaeologically the sociopolitical shift can be seen in the material culture: Elite graves and ceramic sequences of the First Intermediate Period showed strong regional affinities and were replaced with uniform inventory by the late 11th Dynasty, coinciding with the onset of a revitalized central authority. However, a strong sense of provincial identity remained throughout the Middle Kingdom, giving the impression that the central authority was not as thoroughly infused throughout the hinterland areas as it was in the Old Kingdom. The ceramic sequences and other forms of cultural expressions again separate into provincial styles by the first half of the 13th Dynasty, when central authority was again weak.

THE ENVIRONMENTAL EVIDENCE

The archaeologist Barbara Bell has postulated that the unsettled conditions described in the texts at the beginning of the First Intermediate Period were brought on by disastrously low Nile floods. This she determined by correlating geological events with textual evidence. For example, she equates a passage attributed to Ankhtifi, who notes that he fed Hefat (Mo 'Alla) at a time when the sky was in clouds and the land was in the wind, with a report by the geologist Karl Butzer that windblown sand choked off the canal leading from the Nile to the Fayum lake sometime after the Old Kingdom, and that nearly two meters of sediments were winnowed away from cemeteries at Hierakonpolis near the end of Dynasty 6. According to Bell, the wind and blowing sands required to deflate the Hierakonpolis cemetery and fill the canal supported Ankhtifi's comment that the "land was in the wind." The evidence, although highly suggestive, remains inconclusive because of a lack of accurate dating.

More recently, however, Bell's findings have received further support from geologists working in the Delta, Fayum, and the Oases. In the Fayum, examination of lake-bottom sediments by geoarchaeologist Fekri Hassan revealed a surprising inconsistency: a lack of Old Kingdom lake deposits. This he suggests is because the lake had dried up sometime after the Old Kingdom and the deposits were winnowed away by arid winds. This correlates well with Butzer's finds that the canal connecting the Nile to the Fayum was choked off by wind-blown sands.

In the Delta, a team of scientists led by Jean-Daniel Stanley noticed a distinct thin layer of reddish-brown silt dating between 2250 to 2050 BC concurrent with the time of the collapse of the Old Kingdom. This layer indicated that the Delta floodplain had been dry for a long period of time, allowing reddish-brown iron oxides to accumulate at the surface, giving the silt its distinctive coloring.

There is also compelling evidence of dry conditions in other parts of Egypt. For example, encroaching desert sands engulfed the Old Kingdom capital at Memphis during the First Intermediate Period, forcing its inhabitants to move activities to the south and east. A similar phenomenon was also observed farther north at Abu Roash as well as in other areas far removed from the Old Kingdom delta. Investigations at 'Ayn Asil in Dakhla Oasis, for example, reveal a progressive silting of the site by the end of the Old Kingdom, with more than four meters of windblown sand being deposited there, forcing the site to be abandoned. The Fayum Lake's missing deposits, the Delta's red soil, and the increased aeolian activity also correlate to a dry climatic episode in Ethiopia and equatorial Africa (2200–2100 BC), the source of the Nile floods.

If environmental factors did indeed contribute to the downfall of the Old Kingdom, we might see similar correlations at other periods of sociopolitical upheaval in Egypt. That is, can our model predict a similar cultural response for another occurrence under similar conditions? Looking for such a correlation in Egypt's Second Intermediate Period thus seems an appropriate test.

CORRELATION OR CAUSATION

Concurrent with the reestablishment of central authority in Dynasty 12, a number of ancient records note the resumption of "good" or at least consistent Nile floods. Scholars have estimated that average Middle Kingdom floods returned to heights similar to that of today. Sometime at the end of the First Intermediate Period, ancient Lake Moeris in the Fayum also returned to pre-drought levels, estimated to be around 18 meters above sea level.

Returning to Egypt's sociopolitical framework, with the onset of "normal" Nile floods central authority seems to have resumed for some 250 years, ending with the Second Intermediate Period. The Second Intermediate Period is defined as the time Egypt was under divided rule, commencing in the last fifty years of the 13th Dynasty with the rise of non-Egyptian rulers in the east Delta. The total collapse of political authority, however, did not come until the Syro-Palestinian rulers called Hyksos usurped the throne (ca. 1650 BC) and held it for about 100 years, even though an indigenous political administration continued in Thebes and eventually pushed out the Hyksos by force of arms in the late 17th Dynasty.

As with the First Intermediate Period, there is speculation that a deteriorating environment might have contributed to the loss of central authority and the onset of the Second Intermediate Period. This time, however, defining the role of climatic stress is more complicated. During the latter part of the Middle Kingdom, Bell believes the average flood levels were overall higher than those of the New Kingdom, which had levels comparable to those of modern times. Abhorrent floods measuring some three to four times higher than the highest flood of modern times are postulated for a period of a few decades in the Middle Kingdom, but floods of high magnitude were also recorded across the reigns of Amenemhet III and his four successors. As the floods receded to New Kingdom levels, Egyptians had to readjust their water regulating system and its canals and dikes to the new lower levels. Whether this happened slowly or over a period of a decade no one is certain, but the loss of central authority in the Second Intermediate Period is correlated with reduction in flood heights.

Here again Bell has proposed that a series of extremely low floods correlated with textual records of a famine. Nevertheless, although famines are recorded during this period, they do not seem as numerous as those of the First Intermediate Period, and the weakening of central authority was not really a collapse but more of a simple fading away until power once again rested in the hands of provincial rulers. What was the stimulus for the Asiatic migrations, such as the Hyksos, into Egypt, however, remains an important archaeological question.

In Palestine, the archaeological record provides a fairly clear indication of cultural and environmental change at the end of the Early Bronze Age. [In Palestine, the end of the Old Kingdom corresponds to the end of the Early Bronze Age (EB III–IV) and the end of the Middle Kingdom with the Middle Bronze Age (MB II–III).] Most interesting is the discovery that settlements in Cis-Jordan, for the most part, do not survive into the subsequent transitional phase from the Early to Middle Bronze Age, and a movement is detectable from large fortified tells to smaller centers. In many cases the larger population centers seem to have been simply abandoned. It is clear that there is a cultural continuum between EB III and EB IV, but there is a marked change in the economy of the society. In place of the semi-industrialized society of EB III, which included international trade, is rustic pastoralism, in which stockbreeding supersedes agriculture as the guiding force of day-to-day life.

That the abandonment of settlements in favor of pastoralism was more than an isolated incident is corroborated by the work of Bill Devers, who excavated a Negev settlement of EB IV age at Bir Resim and found similar evidence.

The environmental conditions of Syro-Palestine in MB II–III, as with those in contemporary Egypt, do not seem so severe as those of Egypt's First Intermediate Period and Palestine's Early Bronze Age. However, there is evidence, albeit spotty, of climatic deterioration in parts of modern central Israel and the Jordanian Highlands that undoubtedly affected the human inhabitants of the region in Middle Bronze times. What is known is that peoples of the area during this period retained a dispersed settlement pattern and seemingly wandered in search of new grazing lands.

That pastoral nomadism was widespread across the region at this time suggests that environmental conditions reduced the carrying capacity of the land. Evidence for this is the decline of sedentary agriculture and the onset of an expansion of nomadic pastoralism in Palestine in the Middle to Late Bronze Age. At the same time the agricultural retreat opened new pastures to herders as land went fallow. Some have suggested that literally half the region's population turned to pastoral pursuits. This dramatic increase in the number of pastoralists produced a need to expand across larger territory, and conflict between nomadic groups as well as between the nomadic pastoralists and sedentary peoples resulted.

With many peoples on the move, certainly some, perhaps many, were drawn to Egypt's delta, which even under drought conditions offered pastoralists of the day better grazing than the hinterlands of Palestine. As early as the Old Kingdom, Asiatics were settling in the Eastern Delta in ever-increasing numbers as the weakened central government lost its ability to control the borders. One must suppose that with the fall of central authority in Egypt, this influx continued unabated.

Does the cultural and environmental evidence prove that Egypt's First and Second Intermediate periods were a response to deteriorating regional conditions? Unfortunately, no. Sadly, in archaeology, there are few proven truths; rather, we must settle for confirmed hypotheses and models that stand as conditional truths until shown to be incorrect or in need of further embellishment.

Although there exists a growing body of evidence for a changing environment during the Middle Kingdom and Intermediate periods, archaeologists still must establish a stronger relationship between these events and the changing sociopolitical scene of Egypt and Southwest Asia. A correlation of environmental events does not, in and of itself, mean causation. More archaeological work is needed, particularly in the area of environmental archaeology, in both cemeteries and settlements of the period. Regional analysis too is integral in understanding the overall impact of climatic variation and its effect on the riverine environment and the ancient inhabitants of the valley.

8

THE DESERT FRONTIERS: ARCHAEOLOGY OF THE "OTHER"

I destroyed the Seirites of the clans of the Shasu people. I plundered their tent camps of people and possessions and their cattle likewise, they being without number, they being bound and carried way as captives as tribute of Egypt...

(Papyrus Harris I, 76, lines 9–11)

We have finished passing the tribes of the Shasu of Edom (Transjordan) through the fortress Merneptah-content with peace, which is (in) Tjekku to go to the pools of the house of Atum... for their sustenance and the sustenance of their flocks, by the will of pharaoh...

(Papyrus Anastasia IV, 18, lines 6–7)

Desert-dwelling peoples have a long history in Egypt, dating from the Paleolithic period to modern times. Although some of these people lived within the boundaries of what we would consider Egyptian territory, they were, as are today's modern counterparts, perceived as being something other than Egyptian. During the Dynastic period many names of desert groups are known such as Shasu, Meshwes, and Rebu, and we get the impression that although at times tolerated, they were for the most part considered a nuisance or, as with the Hyskos, reviled. Archaeologically we know little about these nomadic desert peoples who lived for the most part just outside of Egypt's sphere of control and only occasionally ventured into Egypt proper (at least until the 19th Dynasty). This lack of knowledge is in large part because of the very manner in which they lived: A lifestyle not easily visible to archaeology. Some have even gone so far as to suggest that archaeology is an ineffective tool when dealing with the ephemeral remains of nomads.

Fortunately, such statements are simply not true. The ancient nomadic peoples did leave traces of their passage; the problem is that most archaeologists working in Egypt have been trained in settlement archaeology and are accustomed to dealing with village and town sites of some historical depth. Archaeological remains left by nomadic peoples are often of low density and do not extend over large areas. Ethnographic accounts show that many modern Bedouin sites cover no more than 10 square meters and possess only a few pottery sherds, or discarded food tins and a fire hearth. Researching such sites clearly requires a different set of techniques than those applied in the Nile Valley – techniques more akin to those practiced by Paleolithic archaeologists who emphasize regional survey and representative sampling.

In an attempt to better understand ancient desert dwellers and their archaeological imprint, scholars have turned to studying modern Bedouin and the ethnographic records of historic nomadic pastoralists, their sites, and the processes that affected them. The study of modern pastoralists and their material remains to gain insights into the behavioral realm of ancient pastoralists is a practice referred to as behavioral archaeology, or more commonly, ethnoarchaeology.

Ethnoarchaeology is a branch of archaeology that employs ethnographic data to assist in the understanding of the archaeological record. Ethnography can tell us much about nomadic behavior in general, and ethnoarchaeology can provide important background against which the archaeological remains of ancient nomads and pastoralists can be examined. In practice, ethnographic data is compared to archaeologically derived hypotheses and models not so much to affirm or negate their probability, but to augment and refine the model for archaeological testing. However, although ethnographic studies can provide insights into past practices, it cannot be used as a looking glass into ancient behavior: All pastoral nomads are not the same. Today's nomadic pastoralists represent a subset of what once was a much larger and more diverse lifestyle; therefore, modern nomadic peoples do not represent all the behaviors and activities carried out by earlier groups. The role of ethnoarchaeology is not so much to create an explanation through analogy as it is to elucidate the processes that formed the extant record and the inherent variability therein.

Theoretically, ethnoarchaeology does assume that behavioral elements of a sociocultural system have material correlates that are incorporated into the archaeological record. If these patterns are recognizable in the archaeological record, they can be used to develop inferences about the behaviors with which they were associated. They cannot prove what behaviors existed in the past but they can define relationships between behavior and material culture that allow archaeologists to better understand the variables related to the patterns in material remains that are recovered. It is up to the archaeologist to then deduce the past as it is reflected in those remains.

Applying these concepts to real data, however, does require that some very practical issues be considered. For example, ethnography documents short-term change, yet archaeology is best equipped to monitor long-term processes. Even our most relied-upon method of dating, C-14, has an error factor larger than the period of time covered by most ethnographic studies. Perhaps most important is the fact that today's cultures are but a small subset of what has existed in the past, and no correlation can be considered a validation of past behavior. Correlations can, however, provide insight.

For example, in one study Byzantine/early Arab Bedouin sites were contrasted against modern Bedouin pastoralists living in the same region to better understand their differences with respect to group size and labor investment in domestic activities such as architecture and agriculture. A regional survey identified some 165 modern Bedouin campsites where site location, material remains, definition, and location of the task areas (e.g., animal pens, refuse areas, or living quarters) were documented. Also, a number of sites were periodically revisited to observe the changes that occurred over time.

The researchers found that within the first few years after a tent encampment was abandoned, it was still easily recognizable at some distance because of the contrast in soil color, probably because of the fire ash and animal dung deposited at the site. In fact, during the flowering season (February to April) the abandoned animal pens were covered in blooms, no doubt a response to the dung-enriched soil.

Where a tent had been placed was also easily identified because the area was usually still clear of stones, and it was often possible to trace the rectangular shape of the tent by the shallow drainage channels dug around it. Occasionally, the rocks used to fix the tent cloth in place were still in a continuous line. Within the former tent boundary stood the remains of fire hearths, and occasionally, a crude, stone-paved area was found near a corner of the tent.

Modern Bedouin camps tended to be concentrated in small groups on the higher elevations of valley floors and wadi terraces. These sites were protected from winter flooding and prevailing winds. Tent entrances always faced the east or southeast, presumably to protect against the regular westerly winds. On occasion up to fifteen sites were found in an area of less than one square kilometer. Because the usual encampment consisted of one or two tents and some animal enclosures, site clusters probably represent repeated visits to the same area. In addition to the tent encampments, sites of an even more ephemeral nature were found at higher elevations. These were thought to be simple herding camps occupied very briefly by a few individuals. A number of storage installations were found in addition to the inhabited camps. These facilities, built on cliffs and slopes using locally available materials, were used to store items such as grain and tools over long periods.

Unlike modern Bedouin tent encampments, Byzantine/early Arab Bedouin sites were characterized by round and elliptical dwellings (approx. 3–8 meters in diameter) made of local stone. Usually each dwelling unit had one or two rooms attached to a courtyard, within which were found fireplaces and cooking installations. The walls were built to a height of 0.5–1.2 meters and the roof was made of lighter perishable materials or tent cloth. Most of the structure had openings facing toward the south or southeast, away from the prevailing winds common to the area. Apart from the dwellings, the sites also contained round or ovoid enclosures about 8–20 meters in diameter, which were probably used to hold herd animals (Figure 8.1).

As with the Bedouin of today, most of the ancient sites were built on wadi terraces well protected from wind, but unlike modern sites, which accommodated only one or two tent shelters, some of the ancient sites held ten, twenty, or more structures. The settlements were not uniform in size or in the number of structures. Sites of one-to-three structures and large concentrations of ten or more structures were documented. Also found were a number of sites with no architectural remains. These were identified only by concentrations of ceramics, lines of stones, and 0.2–1.0 meter round features. It seems that these were ephemeral camps, perhaps representing those involved in pastoral herding.

When comparing the Byzantine/early Arab to modern Bedouin sites, the types of artifacts naturally differ; the modern sites yield food tins, spent batteries, plastics, and other items of the modern world, whereas the ancient sites are composed mostly of pottery and architectural features. Both modern and historic groups share the same location on valley floors and low terraces. Reasons for choosing these preferred locations were similar: access to water and pasture, and protection from the prevailing winds. In some cases, the modern Bedouin would even camp within the walls of the ancient Byzantine/early Arab homes to help protect their tents against the elements. In the dumps and refuse areas of both modern and ancient sites, sheep and goat bones were found in abundance.

The respective domestic structures perhaps represent the greatest difference between the groups. The Byzantine/early Arab structures of stone, sometimes in groups of ten or more, suggest a more sedentary lifestyle with access to more resources than the tent-dwelling Bedouin of today. This also reflects a difference in time and labor investment. Ancient Byzantine/early Arabs constructed homes, animal pens, and most notably terraces for agriculture. Aside from making repairs to ancient wells or augmenting an ancient house structure to accommodate a tent, modern Bedouin did little construction. Although they did occasionally engage in agriculture, they always used the ancient terraced field system, never preparing new ones or even extending the old ones. It seems investing in agriculture is not an important factor in modern Bedouin life.

FIGURE 8.1. A Byzantine/Early Arab period Bedouin campsite. (Courtesy of Steven Rosen).

Interestingly, as the authors of the study point out, in neighboring regions such as the southern Sinai, Bedouin did make more permanent domestic structures similar to those of the Byzantine/early Arabs and practiced a more sedentary lifestyle, splitting their time between the lowlands during the winter and the higher, cooler elevations in the summer. This more settled lifestyle was attributed, it was believed, to higher amounts of effective precipitation. Scholars have speculated, therefore, that the differences in labor investments seen between Byzantine/early Arab and modern Bedouins reflect an environmental shift to more arid conditions and a cultural adaptation whereby investing in agriculture and sedentism was no longer a viable strategy – certainly a testable hypothesis for future research.

As previously stated, the central problem in using ethnoarchaeological data is the extent to which we are able to correlate archaeological evidence of nomadic peoples to behavior, using modern analogs. The example given above is a relatively straightforward comparison with logical conclusions. How would the conclusions stand if our environmental supposition could not be verified and the cultures were separated by several thousand years?

In exploring the identity of the ancient frontier cultures, what we do know is that people such as the Shasu and Meshwes were by most accounts nomadic pastoralists. Our knowledge, however, is limited almost exclusively to texts, reliefs, and monuments of the 18th and 19th dynasties and if not for these sources, we would have virtually no record of them. (There are earlier references dating to the Predynastic Period and more solid evidence dating to Dynasty 5.)

Philologists have provided us with some additional evidence. They note that the name *Shasu* is likely derived from the Egyptian verb *shas*, which basically meant to move on foot (it was also used in the context of journeys and of the daily motion of the sun). As early as the 5th Dynasty, a form of the word was applied to wanderers that the Egyptians habitually came into contact with in the Sinai and Canaan, and it rapidly became a term with cultural implications. The resultant *shasw* or Shasu came to be used in ways similar to our word *Bedu* or *Bedouin*. Two texts provide information on Shasu culture: A school text (the Papyrus Anastasia VI 51–61) reports a typical nomadic pastoral situation dominated by small livestock (sheep and goats). From the Papyrus Harris (I 76, 9–11), we learn that the Shasu lived in tents, were socially organized by families (tribes?), and possessed mostly small livestock for subsistence.

Although the Shasu seem to have maintained a constant presence along Egypt's borders, they were little more than a thorn in the Pharaoh's side until just before the beginning of the 19th Dynasty, when they established themselves in the Negev and northern Sinai, essentially cutting off Egypt's trade routes to the east. Though Seti I had little trouble in beating them back, texts report the Shasu, more than once, along the Suez frontier moving their livestock to their seasonal pasturage near the Wadi Tumilat. References to "the Shasu of the inverted water" and the Shasu settlements in Middle Egypt at Atfih and Spermeru suggest they also trekked south through the Eastern Desert, entered the Nile Valley, and settled across from the Fayum.

The Shasu were not the only eastern nomads with which Egypt had to contend. According to Rothenberg, the central and southern regions of Sinai were inhabited since Paleolithic times by peoples originating from the Arabian Peninsula, northeast Asia, and Egypt. Scholars have defined three archaeological phases for the region (Elatian, Timnian I and II), which are roughly contemporaneous with Egypt's Badarian, Naqada II, and Early Dynastic periods. In addition to these more settled cultures, itinerant caravan traders, the Sabi and Sala, are also known to have camped in the area as they traversed the region, transporting among other things the Red Sea shells so coveted for jewelry and crafts. Textual records from the time of Cambyses also speak of the troglodytes of the Eastern Desert. Eight groups were known, two of which were the Therothoae (those who run down beasts) and the Ichthyophagi (fish eaters) of the Red Sea coastal area. Troglodytes are also represented in the 12th Dynasty tomb of Senbi at Meir. Some have suggested that these peoples roamed from Suez to far southern Sudan and are perhaps ancestral to the Ababda and the Bisharin Bedouin of today.

The Western Desert, unlike the Eastern regions, seems to have offered very little in the way of exploitable resources. With the exception of oases and the Mediterranean coast, large settlements seem to have been nearly impossible to sustain. Nevertheless, there are references to groups of people living west of the Nile from the beginning of the Dynastic period. *Libya* is the general term used to refer to the region, although Egyptians regarded the term more as a designate for the people than the land.

Egyptian sources mention the presence of Libyans inhabiting Western Desert oases, which provided a series of rest stops for watering and trading along a desert trail extending from Egypt into the Sudan. This trade route, however, never received the same level of attention as those leading to Asia. It is not until the end of the 18th Dynasty that there is evidence of imports from the Western Desert and even then they are of modest quantities, dominated by cattle products, ostrich eggs and feathers, and some mercenaries. With limited economic opportunities or military threat (at least until the 19th Dynasty), the Western Desert seemed more a barrier than a corridor.

It is clear from texts that the Egyptians did recognize different groups of Libyans, of which the most commonly referred to, at least in the New Kingdom, were Tjemehu, Tjehenu, Meshwesh, and Rebu (or Libu), each of whom were characteristically depicted in art. *Tjemehu* and *Tjehenu* were very ancient terms that originally referred to the inhabitants of the regions known as Tjemeh and Tjehnu; the former seemingly bordered the Nile Delta, the latter extended farther southwards. Although these terms originally referred to specific areas, by New Kingdom times they seem to have become more generic and could be applied to the whole region west of the Delta as far as Cyrenaica in modern Libya. For example, the Merneptah invasion text contains the line, "*the land of Tjehnu came... and it consisted of Libu, Seped* (a minor Libyan group) *and Meshwesh....*"

The Meshwesh and Rebu are thought to have come from somewhere west of Tjemeh and Tjehnu. This is indicated by the records of the attempted invasions under Merneptah and Ramesses III that state these two groups descended upon the Tjehnu before reaching Egypt. Exactly where to the west these groups might have originated is not clear. Because of their sudden appearance in the records, it has been suggested that they may have arrived in North Africa from a location far to the west or southwest of modern Libya. However, they may well have been there all along. Their sudden appearance may simply represent increased activity by these groups and/or a growing awareness of this region by the Egyptians.

An interesting social model proposed by O'Connor is that the Rebu and Meshwesh had reached a certain stage in their political and social development that led them to attempt to expand and settle into Egyptian territory. This would have been motivated by the desire of a developing elite to advance their status and to allow the exploitation of the conquered people and their land. New territory would also provide a base for the plundering of other nearby lands. That the Meshwesh and Rebu possessed a stratified society as required by this model is illustrated in the records of Merneptah and Ramesses III, where their chiefs and systems of government can be discerned to a certain extent. Unfortunately, although certainly a possible explanation for increasing hostility, to substantiate it archaeologically would require significant research on a number of sites to determine the existence of a significant population, and evidence that that population was hierarchically organized to the level of being able to direct a conflict for reasons of territorial expansion.

NOMADS AND ARCHAEOLOGY

How might one approach such a problem when nomadic peoples are the subjects? So little is actually known about the "other" of Egypt that just to find archaeological evidence of their presence would be significant. Who were these people, how did they live, from where did they come, were any indigenous, were they immigrants or offshoots of neighboring groups, how large were their communities, and were they hierarchically arranged? These are just a few of the questions one can pose about these little-known peoples.

Looking out over the large open deserts of Egypt (Figure 8.2), it is clear that without some special insights, finding archaeological sites would be difficult. First and foremost the Meshwesh, Shasu, and others were nomadic pastoralists and by definition moved. Thus any archaeological investigation must consider the dynamic nature of the ancient nomadic system and understand that any site is only a single expression of a larger social system extending over a large territory. Clearly to better understand the ancient nomads requires a "regional" rather than "site" perspective. In practical terms, this means that surveys must target site diversity across a region and therefore cover large expanses of terrain.

Herein lays the problem, implementation; finding evidence of small ephemeral encampments within a vast area. Those techniques (presented in earlier chapters) designed to investigate the sparse far-flung assemblages of Paleolithic hunter-gatherers, which focused on regional surveys, representative sampling, and collecting, would serve well in these circumstances. This does, however, constitute a daunting task unless some means can be found to increase the chances of discovery. One way is to stratify the study area.

FIGURE 8.2. An example of Egypt's vast desert regions (photo by D. J. Brewer).

If we assume the nomadic peoples living on Egypt's frontiers were pastoralists, and their mobile lifestyle was dictated by the necessities of their herd's need for forage and water, we may be able to predict where herd animals might have been sustained, and thereby increase the possibility of locating and exploring these people's ancient pastoral sites.

(c)

FIGURE 8.2 (*continued*)

Ruminants (cud-chewing animals) such as cattle, sheep, and goats transfer otherwise unusable plants into edible products and therefore serve as a portable resource. In Egypt, the forage and grasses needed to sustain herd animals grew in a variety of areas, and depending on the availability of water could be tall and lush or sparse, dry, and stunted. The productivity of grazing lands, however, would have varied from year to year due to the vagaries of Egypt's rainfall. Consequently, a grazing strategy would have to evolve that would acceptably counter the local constraints and meet the needs of the herds – that is, a nomadic lifestyle.

Cattle are perhaps the most demanding of the ancient herd animals, requiring water on almost a daily basis. Like cattle, sheep are grazing ungulates but require less water. Goats, on the other hand, are browsers and adapt well to particularly harsh environments; they are perhaps the most versatile of all ruminants in their feeding habits, a factor that has greatly influenced their success as a staple of nomadic pastoralists. They have a wider tolerance of habitat types, relative to sheep and cattle: They are able to feed and breed on a minimum of food and under extremes of temperature and humidity. Goats also complement a flock of sheep or cattle by browsing on thorny scrubland whereas the sheep and cattle graze on grasses.

Ethnoarchaeological studies of modern pastoralists in the Sahel show that only the areas receiving at least 500 millimeters of seasonal rainfall are considered to be good for cattle; areas receiving 300–400 millimeters are adequate for sheep, and cattle can be raised if water and diet supplements are available; areas with 100–200 millimeters are suitable for sheep and goats and areas with fewer than 100 millimeters can support only goats (and camels). Given the available ecological data, it seems extremely improbable that the Eastern Sahara could have received more than 400 millimeters of rain per annum in the Dynastic period, limiting cattle pastoralists to oases and coastal areas where water and forage requirements could be met. Sheep and certainly goats, however, could have thrived in a number of regions.

Such regions might be identified by searching ancient texts and modern environmental maps and satellite photos. Interestingly, while working on a completely unrelated problem, I noticed that an important soil type found on the Nile's floodplain is also found in certain parts of the Eastern Desert. This soil type (calcareous fluvisols, here noted as Jc soils, see Figure 8.3) is significant because it is associated with agriculture along the river, but in the desert it would have produced grazing lands after episodic rains.

In every large wadi where rock art depicting pastoral animals has been identified, Jc soils are present. In wadis that do not have Jc soils, archaeological evidence is lacking or at least rarely observed. One might hypothesize then that Jc soil areas were preferred pastoral habitats and therefore would be promising areas to explore for further evidence of ancient pastoralists. Confounding our hypothesis, however, is the fact that many Jc soil areas seem to correlate with known trade corridors between the Red Sea and Nile Valley (Figure 8.3). This begs the question: Were these wadis just transit corridors, or were they part of a subsistence strategy for nomadic peoples, or both? If they were simply transit corridors, then our opportunities for finding domestic encampments might be diminished, but perhaps they also served as grazing lands. What is needed to test the predictive model and create a systematic means for locating archaeological sites is to survey Jc soil areas that were not passages between the Red Sea and Nile Valley. Toward this goal, two internal drainage basins were selected for survey based on satellite images and soil maps. These basins were chosen because they did not serve as likely passes between the Nile and Red Sea, and they possess Jc soils.

If evidence for ancient herders were found in internal drainage basins, it would strengthen the validity of the soil's predictive model and lend credence to our hypothesis that ancient Bedouin-type peoples were not simply transiting through the desert but lived in and pastured their herds in those areas where they could be sustained.

As is common in archaeology, what was found differed from what we set out to find. The Jc soil survey showed rock art to be found in all areas with Jc soils,

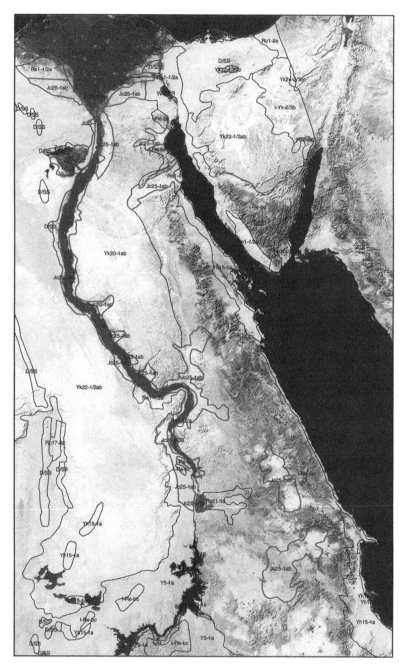

FIGURE 8.3. Distribution of calcareous fluvisols (or Jc soils) in Egypt. When located in desert environs, these soils would have offered pasturage after periodic rains (Digital Soil Map of the World ver. 3.6, 2003).

and the amount of art was proportional to the size of the Jc soils area – the larger the area, the more art. We were, however, unable to find any evidence of other artifactual materials such as lithics, pottery, or even fire hearths. We now had to ask why. Perhaps our field methods were not appropriately designed to locate such sites? To cross-check our field methods against the evidence, or lack thereof, a survey was conducted about 550 kilometers north of the study area along the Wadi Araba and its tributaries. Although only a few examples of rock art were noted, several Neolithic, Predynastic, and later period sites were found. The sites were identified by lithic scatters and broken pottery. The Neolithic as well as the Predynastic sites tended to be located on high terraces overlooking the wide wadi plane; the later sites were found on the wadi plane itself. These discoveries reinforced our confidence that our field techniques were adequate and that some other reason may explain the lack of similar type sites in our Jc soil areas.

That little rock art was found in the Wadi Araba survey is not surprising. The northern half of the Eastern Desert is limestone, which weathers poorly, and in fact, relatively few examples of rock art come from this area. On the other hand, wadi passes through the Red Sea Mountains in the southern half of Egypt have produced myriad examples of rock art, at least in part because these mountain passes are of hard igneous rock, a more stable "canvas" for ancient artists. The lack of artifact material near the Jc art sites may be due to the fact that many areas near the art were covered by drifting sand, but this certainly was not the case for all sites. Perhaps, as with Wadi Araba, the sites we seek are not located in the Jc soil areas on the floor of ravines and valleys, but on the terraces above, where a person can oversee the activities below.

Interpreting the evidence in hand (the rock art), the work of archaeologist Oliver Myers and art historian Hans Winkler stand out as early attempts to understand the desert cultures through their art. Myers did some amazing things for the time. It is clear from his fieldwork in the Western Desert that he collected artifacts he felt were associated with rock art, and he took the precaution of digging and collecting from the same-sized areas in many of his sites. Unfortunately, we do not know what Myers collected because no report was ever published. What we do know is that Myers discovered chipped stone tools, some stone circles thought to be tent rings, milling stones, and pottery. The material (notes and artifacts) now held at the Museum of Man in France was studied in 1971 by William McHugh. From his study, McHugh felt the Western Desert artifacts dated to around 6000–4000 BCE.

Unfortunately, the Eastern Desert sites have yet to produce datable materials, other than the rock art, which is notoriously difficult to date with any precision. The dating of rock art depends on a number of clues such as:

(1) the internal composition of the picture (are extinct animals or datable artifacts shown?);
(2) the presence of dated inscriptions;
(3) the overlapping and cross-cutting relationships of different styles or themes (does one type of representation consistently overlie another?), and
(4) general stylistic trends and patterns of artistic development (is there a consistent trend toward the stylization of motifs?).

Winkler collected and classified rock drawings from forty different sites and grouped the scenes into five periods, in many cases attempting to connect particular art styles with particular peoples:

(1) Arab;
(2) Greco-Roman-Coptic;
(3) Dynastic;
(4) Undatable early Predynastic and prehistoric in the Eastern Desert, and
(5) Undatable early Predynastic and prehistoric in the Western Desert.

Winkler divided categories 4 and 5 into cultural groups: (a) autochthonous mountain dwellers, (b) early Nile dwellers, (c) eastern invaders, and (d) earliest hunters. In an attempt to breathe life into his subjects, Winkler described each group in terms of its major cultural characteristics, such as fauna, weapons, hunting practices, boats, social life, and religion. He even went so far as to propose ethnic divisions based on costume and comparisons with modern peoples of the area.

Of course, by modern anthropological standards Winkler's ethnographic analogies were not adequately controlled and he almost certainly pushed interpretation beyond the evidence at hand. Nevertheless, he did uncover some real differences in desert rock art – differences that indicated a considerable passage of time. The most ancient rock-drawings were quite distinct from those that came later. Animals, game traps, footprints of game, and geometrical designs were standard motifs. He believed the earliest hunters lived along the Nile; as evidence he gave pictures of the crocodile. Additionally, these hunters possessed the bow and the dog.

Winkler believed these early hunters were succeeded by cattle pastoralists, who he referred to as autochthonous mountain dwellers. Although the rock drawings suggested to Winkler that the mountain dwellers (i.e., cattle pastoralists) still hunted wild animals such as ibex, antelope, and ostrich, he thought that the most commonly depicted animals – long-horned cattle – were thoroughly domesticated as demonstrated by artificial deformation of the horns and by the care applied to representations of the udder, indicating to him that the artists appreciated milk. Because cattle pictures excel in the care applied to them, Winkler thought it reflected their importance in ancient society. Also, people shown hunting cattle with bow and arrow suggested to him that wild cattle still existed in the region.

A comparison of the frequency of animals depicted in the scenes led McHugh to conclude that engraved hunting scenes preceded the painted pastoral scenes. In his analysis, he stresses that the paintings and engravings tabulated by Winkler are significantly different in the species represented. Although cattle are most abundant in both categories, they comprise almost 98 percent of the animals depicted in Winkler's series of painted scenes as compared with only 32 percent in his series of engravings. On the other hand, wild animals (excluding canids) comprise 62 percent of all animals in the engraved scenes but only 2 percent of those in the painted scenes. McHugh's conclusions are supported by findings in eastern Chad, where engraved hunting scenes also seem to precede painted pastoral motifs in both the Ennedi and Tibesti massifs.

The rock art discovered through our Jc soil survey included incised and pecked scenes but no painted examples. Comparing them to Winkler's classification scheme as well as using datable signs and subjects within the scenes, we find that the Jc rock art ranged from Predynastic to the Arab period and in many instances, pictures from vastly different periods were located directly adjacent to one another (Figure 8.4). Contrary to observations made by earlier scholars, there did not seem to be any correlation between mode of manufacture (pecking or incising) and age: scenes from any period could be pecked or incised. The subject matter and manner or style of representation, however, did differ somewhat from Winker's Western Desert scenes. Whereas some scenes mimicked the illustrations found on Predynastic ceramics (boats, geometric designs), other pictures featuring game animals and hunters correlate most closely with rock art documented in the Negev.

In fact the Negev art looks so similar to some of the Eastern Desert art that it would be hard to separate them if we only view the representations (for example, compare illustrations in Anati 1999 to Winkler 1938–1939 and Redford and Redford 1989). It is not too far a stretch to say that the peoples inhabiting the two areas (Negev and Eastern Desert) shared certain affinities, at least in the metaphysical sense. How much they shared beyond their artistic symbolism is difficult to say without some clearly associated sites and artifacts. Historical records and personal conversations with Eastern Desert Bedu indicate that at

FIGURE 8.4. Example of rock art from the Eastern Desert showing more than one time period represented. Note the patina on the Predynastic renditions of boats, ostriches, ibex, and giraffe, followed by the later-created picture of a man riding a camel (photo by D. J. Brewer).

one time in the not-too-distant past, their range extended around the southern Sinai and into Jordan and Saudi Arabia, but politics intervened and isolated the groups into their respective territories.

Thus, we might speculate and test the premise that at least two ancient Pre/Proto Dynastic era cultures are represented in the rock art associated with Jc soils – a Nile-oriented pastoral group and an indigenous Bedouin group – and both must have utilized the same grazing resources of the Eastern Desert. Whether the Bedouin roamed the area during the same time period or different periods has yet to be determined, but correlates in the Negev would suggest some overlap in time. Those groups represented by Predynastic art motifs seem to possess the same artistic and metaphysical tradition as the developing Naqada culture and therefore may represent that part of society whose responsibility was maintaining herd animals: Later Dynastic texts speak of seasonal cattle drives to better pasturage. The other art tradition can perhaps be attributed to indigenous desert peoples, who ranged across the Eastern Desert into the Sinai and beyond.

9

FROM ARTIFACTS TO CULTURE: BACK TO BASICS

In earlier chapters we discussed sampling, dating, environmental context, and the all-important segregation of artifacts through classification. The problem to consider now is how such data can be structured to help further our understanding of ancient Egyptian society. To do this, the archaeologist must move from an archaeological arrangement of artifacts to a cultural interpretation of those artifacts. In other words, we must interpret culturally what we have defined archaeologically.

How does one make the jump from artifacts to culture interpretation? Frankly, the connection is made by assumption and analogy, albeit following a path established by tradition. Archaeology as a discipline is based on the assumption that the attributes we recognize across a series of artifacts are products of human activity and recur because they are the material remains of ideas held in common by the makers and users of those artifacts. That is, the patterns that we see in pottery, tomb scenes, or architecture reflect ideas and expressions shared by members of the same culture (in our case the ancient Egyptians), and this is why classification plays such a critical role in archaeology: It is the data by which we define the parameters for transitioning from a world of objects to a theoretical world of conjecture. One of the greatest assets for archaeologists working in Egypt is the parallel studies conducted by Egyptologists, which, with their background in art history and philology, add not only tremendous depth to archaeological interpretations but can serve to corroborate or refute our hypotheses and models. In fact, cooperation between the disciplines is paramount to our goals of a fuller understanding of ancient Egypt.

Among the most challenging of Egypt's archaeological sites are the large, multi-component New Kingdom settlements. Although we have seen that the archaeological method works well under many different circumstances, it does have its limitations. Understanding the various interrelated roles of secular, royal, and religious sectors within a large New Kingdom settlement serves as a good example. Archaeological data is best adapted to understanding trends across time, not intricate reconstructions of a particular point in time. Nevertheless, pursuing the same goal through a multidisciplinary partnership has the potential to elucidate a broader and more accurate picture of the past.

Often viewed as Egypt's Golden Age, the New Kingdom was a time of political stability, great prosperity, and significant achievements in art, architecture, and literature. The wealth of the New Kingdom state and the power of its central authority are most evident in the construction of temples, their upkeep, and their maintenance. Temples were major players in the economy of the New Kingdom and had their own revenue source and administrative bureaucracies. As testimony to their importance and place in Egyptian society, holdings for just three important Dynasty 20 temples refer to nearly 97,000 workers. The tremendous amount of food and goods that were offered to the temple god each day and the "salaries" of the many temple workers were derived from more than half-a-million head of cattle, sheep, and goats and nearly 290,000 hectares of land deeded to the temple, tax free, by the king and other pious individuals.

An astute student of archaeology also might notice that a different physical relationship existed between settlements and temples in the New Kingdom. In the Old or Middle Kingdom monumental architecture was kept more or less at the settlement's periphery, usually to the west (think pyramids). Local temples, made of mudbrick, were modest in size and fit within the size range of other mudbrick town buildings. In the New Kingdom, the preferred building material for temples was stone. The temple was a monumental structure built in the middle of town, such that the residents lived in its shadow, and the juxtaposition of the temple and domestic architecture provided a striking comparison, reinforcing the close-but-unequal relationship between gods and mortals.

Why the Egyptians built such huge monumental structures such as New Kingdom temples is a question asked by many admirers of the culture, and one that is not easy to answer. Anthropologists and other social scientists tell us that monumental architecture, from Old Kingdom pyramids to New Kingdom temples, expresses in a public and enduring manner the ability of the king to control the materials, specialized skills, and labor required to create and maintain such structures. In general, the larger and more ornate such buildings are, the more power they express. Evidence suggests that the need to express power through monumental architecture is greatest in the formative stages of early civilizations (note the pyramids of the Third and

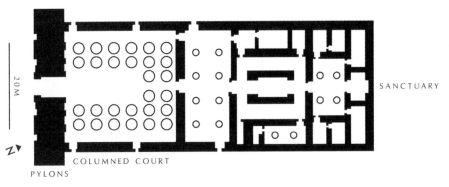

FIGURE 9.1. A typical temple plan of the New Kingdom (Jackie Gardner after Snape 1996).

Fourth dynasties) and in transitional periods when central authority is being reestablished and its rulers are reasserting themselves.

The expansion of the temples, their religious cults, and economic prerogatives are in fact a major theme of the New Kingdom. Temples were renovated and expanded, and new ones founded throughout Egypt, northern Nubia, and the Sinai. The mortuary cult of the ruler himself was celebrated in a royal temple (the mortuary temple) on the west bank at Thebes. As with temples dedicated to the gods, these huge structures had their own endowments and staff of priests, and were part of the elaborate architectural provisions for the king's afterlife.

But why build in such monumental proportions and in the center of the population area and why temples, in the New Kingdom?

THE TEMPLE AS MONUMENT

Combining textual, art historical, and archaeological evidence, it is clear that the entire temple complex was meant to intimidate. Entering a typical New Kingdom temple (Figure 9.1), one passed through two towering pylons that opened to a long straight axial way that led inward through a series of open courts. Along it, the rooms became ever smaller and darker – an effect achieved partly through raised floors and lowered ceilings. The routes' portals were punctuated by magnificently adorned double wooden doors that had both practical utility and intrinsic symbolic power: Closed they excluded intruders, open they admitted the chosen. The axial way through courts and chamber complexes led ultimately to the somewhat cramped private apartment of the god – the sanctuary. Typically constructed over a hillock or symbolic mound, this elevated sanctuary was the mythological center of the universe where the primordial event of creation had occurred. The sanctuary, which held the divine image of the temple god, often made of wood and gilded in gold, was also a portal into the realm of the gods.

Although access to the sanctuary was strictly limited, other parts of the temple were open to pilgrims on special occasions, and many temple rituals were performed for the public. Also, during annual festivals representatives of the populace were ushered into the less-restricted outer courtyards and cere-monial halls of the temple. There, in the role of a congregation or community of adoration, they worshiped the gods, marveled at the temple's splendor, participated in internal processions, and bore witness to the miraculous effect of the secret rites performed within the dark and distant sanctuary, the holy of holies: Rites that piloted the world through various cosmological crises. Temple decorations were intended primarily for gods' eyes but those in public areas were meant for people as well. The small percentage of the populace that was literate could read some of the texts, and everyone could read the artwork.

Temples had formally designated areas located not only at gateways but also in open courtyards, for making supplication and hearing the petitions of gods and men. Temples were equipped with several "portals" (often called false doors) that permitted direct communication between earth, sky, and the netherworld. Ordinary mortals of course could not cross the thresholds but the blessed dead, the living king, and priests could pass through them and into the heavenly world.

As architectural statements, Egyptian temples were symbolic of the land-scape of world order: Obelisks pierced the heavens, flag masts supported the canopy of the sky, pylons mimicked the mountainous horizon, columns held starry ceilings above, and sacred lakes teemed with the life of the primeval swamp. But there was danger in linking heaven and earth and it was, therefore, important to maintain the sanctity of the enveloped temple.

As a religious statement, temples were ritually set apart from the mundane world by consecration of the grounds on which they were erected and by construction of an imposing series of progressively more restrictive walls for protection. The temple's ritual and architectural barriers repulsed the chaotic forces that continually threatened the ordered world within. It was within the temple walls where invisible met visible, the earth met the heavens, and humans interacted with the divine, and keeping world order was the duty of the king.

Clearly, temples were not so much for personal salvation but for maintaining order in the universe. This was accomplished through shared governance between king and god(s), and the temple was the physical embodiment of the cosmic government. The size and splendor of temples reinforced the stature of the king, the gods, and the state, and their presence was an enduring statement of central authority, which in practical terms was a mechanism for maintaining sociopolitical order. The numerous rituals carried out in the temple and the daily offerings were all designed to reinforce this cosmic alliance between king and gods and to maintain order in the spiritual, cosmic, and secular worlds.

Although we do know something about the formal rituals associated with priests, kings, and temples, we still know relatively little about how the populace articulated with the temple on a day-to-day basis in either secular or religious contexts. Complicating such an investigation is that the best place to look for such evidence is at one of Egypt's large New Kingdom sites, which archaeologically speaking, are extremely complicated to work because of the need to control so many variables. Such sites typically stretch for hectares if not kilometers in all directions, and they possess complicated stratigraphy in that areas were used for different purposes over time: Buildings, roads, and paths were built and rebuilt, creating cross-cutting and intrusive features into earlier levels and mixing of time-sensitive artifacts. There is, however, one site where many of the variables associated with a large, temple-dominated community can be controlled: Tell el-Amarna.

In the fifth year of his reign, Akhenaten chose to build a new capital: A city to be built on virgin ground with all the accommodations needed to run the country. Its name was Akhetaten, "The Horizon of the Aten" (modern-day Tell el-Amarna), located roughly halfway between Thebes and Memphis (Figure 9.2). The king's vision for the city was recorded on a series of fourteen tablets known as the Boundary Stele, carved in the cliffs on both sides of the Nile, defining the extent of the settlement (Figure 9.3). Between the boundary steles, Akhetaten encompassed an area of roughly 200 square kilometers (Figure 9.4). What is unique archaeologically about Akhetaten is its short duration of occupation (ca. twenty to twenty-five years), offering the opportunity to explore the workings of a complete city within a narrowly defined span of time. In fact, much of the city's layout is visible on the surface, simplifying sampling design and excavation strategies. The archaeological, textual, and pictorial evidence, combined with the unique circumstances associated with Akhetaten, has provided the opportunity to reconstruct city life in ways not available to archaeology alone.

Although Akhetaten and its temple were in some ways unique, it was in many ways quite traditionally Egyptian. It is doubtful, for example, that building techniques would have differed significantly from those that came before Akhetaten's construction. It is also unlikely that major changes in the

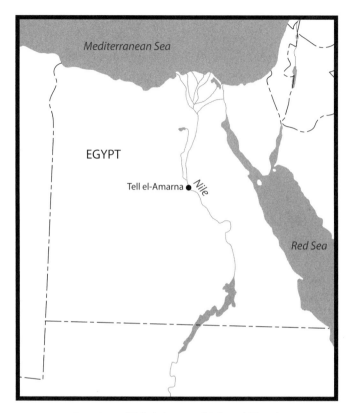

FIGURE 9.2. Location of Tell el-Amarna (Ault and Flores).

general domestic relationship between town and temple or between social strata would have evolved in the five years of Akhenaten's rule prior to the city's construction. Certainly his championing of Atenism influenced aspects of temple design, but all temples exhibit some idiosyncrasies associated with the particular deity they represent. The fact that archaeologists could so readily identify the Aten temple, based on its size, appearance, and quality of construction, eloquently testifies to the existence of its shared characteristics with other period temples as to what a temple should be and how it should appear.

AKHETATEN AND THE ATEN TEMPLE

As always, the particular performance of the cult dictates the form of the building in which the cult ceremonies were performed. Because the predominant deity during the Amarna regime, the Aten, is its own image – the sun disk

BOUNDARY STELAE
(UPPER SECTION)

FIGURE 9.3. An example of a boundary Stele at Tell el Amarna (Jackie Gardner after Davies 1908, pl. XXXIII).

in the sky, with beneficent rays reaching down to earth – it can be worshiped from but not contained within the temple; temple design, therefore, adapted to this aspect of the god. The Aten temple thus differed from traditional New Kingdom temples in that it was an open-air temple made up of congregated buildings separated by open space, not a single coherent structure with annexes, and an axis or path of travel increasingly darkening as one proceeded to the back of the temple and the sanctuary. Although often portrayed as unique, the Aten temple actually shares characteristics with the Old Kingdom sun temples at Abu Gurob, which were open to the sun, and to the altar courts of contemporary mortuary temples.

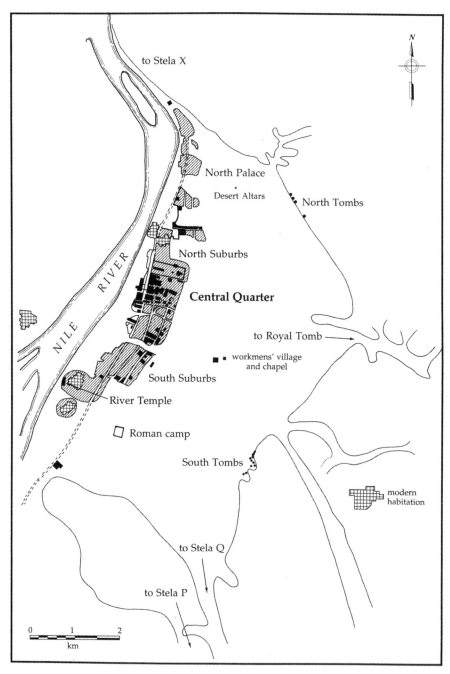

FIGURE 9.4. Map of the city of Akhetaten (after Pendlebury 1951, Brewer and Teeter 2007, figure 4.2).

At Amarna, the main temple (Figure 9.5) was called the Per-Aten, "House of Aten." As with traditional New Kingdom temples, the Aten temple was entered through two immense pylons that opened to a central causeway that ran the entire length of the temple. Immediately after passing though the entrance and located to the north was a columned stone pavilion, followed by the Per-hai, "The House of Rejoicing," a two-columned pavilion flanking either side of the causeway. Passing through the Per-hai, one entered a series of large open-air courts called the Gem-Aten, "The Aten is Found." On either side of the causeway, completely filling the courts, were square offering tables of stone. Even outside the temple proper, near the wall, there were similar altars made of mudbrick. Contemporary tomb scenes show the altars piled with food and drink offerings, the traditional way of serving the gods, but Akhenaten seems to have expanded this feature to excess, perhaps to demonstrate his piety, or more subtly to reflect his closeness to the god Aten and thereby reinforce the appearance of his power. Beyond the third offering court was a series of columns (with offering tables in between), which served as an architectural break, separating the final court and sanctuary from the rest of the temple. The fourth and final court was a virtual field of offering tables numbering in the hundreds, to the east of which lay the sanctuary.

Based on archaeological investigation, it appears this last section of the temple, the sanctuary, was probably the first to be built. At one time there existed a processional way lined by trees leading to the gate of the sanctuary, but the addition of later architectural features has obliterated much of this feature. The entrance into the sanctuary court was elaborate; being on an elevated causeway, it is evident that the approach must have descended to the level of the sanctuary. The forecourt to the sanctuary appeared to hold living quarters similar to those found in a traditional official's home, suggesting it housed priests or other temple functionaries. Tomb scenes show a second court (nearest to the sanctuary chapel) also had rooms, but no archaeological evidence for this exists. Offering tables were placed throughout the courts as indicated by appropriately shaped pits in the sand.

It is thought the sanctuary chapel and altar were open to the sky, conforming to the rest of the temple. It is clear, however, that the visible presence of the sun's disk (i.e., the sun in the sky) did not mean that the performance of the cult ceremony was open to just anyone; tomb scenes from Amarna show that this ceremony was very much the prerogative of the royal family. To the east of the sanctuary were a number of additional buildings and an altar. It is thought a large statue of the king resided here, as well as priestly quarters. How this architectural feature articulated with the sanctuary is uncertain as it

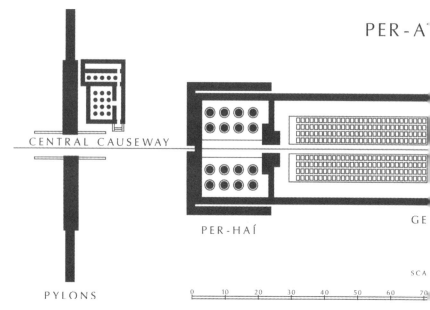

FIGURE 9.5. Diagram of the Aten Temple showing main features presented in the text (Jackie Gardner after Pendlebury 1951).

could only be entered through two doorways on the east temple wall, both of which lay outside the sanctuary itself.

Based on a number of independent lines of evidence, it does not appear as if the temple was ever fully completed. Interestingly a rough blueprint of a temple, perhaps the Aten temple, was discovered in a tomb at Amarna (Figure 9.6). It too supports the archaeological findings that the final form of the temple was never achieved.

From the tomb scenes and the archaeologically derived map of the area, it is clear that as with other New Kingdom communities, the temple at Akhetaten was situated to be a focal point of the city. It was the center of spiritual piety but just as important, it also served as a central point for economic exchange. Beyond the gifts received from various pious callers, the temple was a source of considerable wealth, with agricultural fields and grand herds at its disposal.

Archaeology has shown that the city was dissected by three north-to-south roads crossed at 90-degree angles by smaller roads, creating a roughly gridded area. The three main roads traveled through several well-defined sectors identified as the Central Quarter, the South or Main Suburbs, and the North Suburb. Perhaps the most important of the roads was the so-called "Royal Road." It was the most westerly of the main thoroughfares, running more

TEMPLE

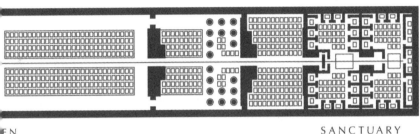

or less parallel with the river. The Royal Road was the "physical" as well as religious arterial road of the community, connecting the governmental areas to all other areas.

The Great Temple, the "House of the Aten my father which I will build in Akhetaten in this place," was probably meant to be the crowning achievement of the entire Amarna venture. With the fall of Akhenaten, the temple was thoroughly destroyed. Not a single block of stone remained in situ: Columns and statues were destroyed, and even the pieces were smashed. In many places it was clear the destroyers went beneath ground level to remove the foundation. Once destruction was complete, clean sand was brought in to seal the temple site from the rest of the world. It is the only instance known from Egypt where a temple was successfully obliterated, leaving only archaeological evidence of its existence.

WHAT IS IN A NAME?

The relative simplicity of Amarna with respect to archaeology, at least when compared to other large New Kingdom settlements, lies in its short duration of occupation. Its areal size and its long history of archaeological investigation, however, do pose additional challenges.

Over time, numerous expeditions have worked the Amarna site. When artifacts or features are named those labels, whether intentional or not, carry

TOMB OF PANEHESY

FIGURE 9.6. A diagramed temple (the Aten Temple?) found in a nearby Amarna period tomb (Jackie Gardner after Davies 1905, pl. XVIII).

meaning. Although this, in and of itself, is not necessarily a bad thing, it can contribute to unintentional results. River Road, Royal Road, and Main Road, as well as other names have been used as referents in Amarna excavation reports for the most westerly north to south road. What do the many names attributed to the different archaeological features at Amarna truly reflect? This is an archaeological conundrum. To record an artifact requires it be labeled, and in cases where something other than a simple alphanumeric system is applied, the artifact or feature may take on attributes of its label (e.g., labeling an object "ax" because it looks like an ax does not make it an ax, it may have served a different purpose). To complicate matters, through the years names change or are abbreviated, creating confusion for later scholars. Listed here are just a few of the names given to several common features at Amarna (Table 9.1). The names lack consistency through time, and certainly their functional implications are points to ponder. For example, researching these very names required repeated readings of the same set of publications just to gain enough confidence to include them in this small table of synonyms. Only by tracing the various descriptions through a trail of publications extending over nearly 100 years was it possible to know what terms were linked with what feature, and the possibility of error still remains.

Renaming a feature – using a different term to describe the same thing or using the same term to describe two different things – is unfortunately,

TABLE 9.1. *Abbreviated list of some named features from Amarna*

Central City
Main City
City Center
North Suburb
North Palace
North City
Riverside Palace
Great Temple
Great Aten Temple
Great Road
Royal Road
River Road
King's Way

a common occurrence in archaeology and can impede understanding by introducing ambiguities into the literature. Although duplication of names for the same object is a matter that can be solved, simple descriptive names can sometimes incur unintended attributes to the artifact or feature.

Archaeologists working in Egypt employ several naming systems that fall into three broad categories: alphanumeric (type a, b, or c), character based (black-topped redware), and functional (bread mold). Functional names are intended to describe in understandable terms objects of the past. Ax, arrowhead, house, and storage room are all commonly used labels that carry with them functional attributes based on our common experience. An object is labeled "ax," "arrowhead" or "storage room" because it looks to us like what an ax, arrowhead, or storage room should look like. The problem is that it may not be an ax, arrowhead, or storage room, but the name sticks, the artifact's function is a product of its descriptive label, and there is no real test to empirically prove its past use. One could look at the wear patterns on the "ax" to see if it had impact marks similar to what would occur if used as an ax, but it also might have been driven into a tree as a step to reach upward for fruit rather than being used to chop down the tree. One could identify a rectangular room with no furnishings as a storage room but it could easily be an empty apartment. Because few valid tests related to terminology use are ever performed, employment of functionally charged labels becomes embedded in the site's archaeological history and through time is regarded as truth.

Clearly, artifact names or labels are of concern because any reconstruction depends on the accuracy of the archaeologist's functional identifications. This is, unfortunately, easier said than done. Corroboration is too often based on common sense and comparative analogy, where enumeration of cognates is equated with substantiation. Not surprisingly, such a system leaves considerable room for error, limiting Egypt's past to the archaeologists' experience and ethnographic knowledge. Amarna suffers from this very type of problem but also serves as an example of how the problem can be corrected: diligence to excavation detail and the study and enumeration of thousands of recovered artifacts.

RECONSIDERING AN ACCEPTED LABEL

Scientific excavations at Amarna have employed functional, descriptive, and alphanumeric labels, and as with many excavations, through the years name changes have occurred. Excavations at Tell el-Amarna began in the 1890s with Flinders Petrie. Epigraphic studies and piecemeal excavations continued through the early part of the twentieth century. In 1926, more extensive work began with Henri Frankfort and later in the 1930s, John Pendlebury conducted a number of excavations at the site. Their early work correctly identified the Central Quarter or Central City as the site of the palace, temple, and government offices (see Figure 9.4). Residential architecture was located in the Central City as well as in separate enclaves, commonly referred to as "suburbs," to the north and south of the administrative quarter. The substantial size of many of the houses in these north and south suburbs suggests that important officials resided there and that there must have been a periodic commute of sorts between the residential and business areas of the site. Another interesting factor of the three main residential areas, judging from the surface remains, was that the north and south suburbs seemed to follow the general haphazard building plan common to Egyptian towns elsewhere. Small, large, and even slum-like structures were all intermixed between a complicated web of streets and paths. The Central City, however, clearly followed a planned grid system. So it seems that although it was not an organically grown community, beyond the central quarter the settlement's architecture and layout was like that of any other period community.

Modern excavations at Amarna have provided a good example of rectifing an error associated with functional labeling of a series of building features. When the area adjacent to the temple wall was originally excavated, many narrow, parallel chambers were discovered, along with numerous broken pieces of pottery. It was determined, based on analogous features at other temples, that the narrow, parallel chambers and associated pottery were indicative of storage rooms and thereafter were labeled "magazines."

FIGURE 9.7. An Egyptian bakery, note the oven, two types of bread and the bread molds (Courtesy of the Brooklyn Museum, http://www.brooklynmuseum.org/ and Ault and Flores after Kemp 1989, figure 96).

In the 1970s, Barry Kemp and his crew reopened excavations in the same area and collected thousands of pieces of broken pottery. The pottery – large, conical-shaped vessels – has come to be known as bread molds, and were presumably used in the baking of bread. Kemp felt, based on his large sample of pottery and his thorough excavation and analysis of the many parallel chambers, that they were not magazines but bakeries.

The bakery complex was composed of more than 100 long parallel chambers, each containing one or more circular ovens of standard domestic design. Bread making itself was depicted in a scene from a reused Amarna block found at Hermopolis (Figure 9.7). The curved roof depicted in the scenes probably represents the vaulted roof of the bakery: There, a man tends an oven in each chamber, and flat round loaves are stacked on a table, as well as long cylindrical bread molds. The scene also depicts the two basic types of bread and bread making: Flat loaves baked on a clay tray and tall narrow loaves baked inside a cylindrical mold. It is fragments of cylindrical "bread molds" that were found all over the desert behind the bakery and, in fact, buried the bakery. The long conical bread loaves were often associated with celebration, particularly religious ones. The fact that the bakeries abut against not only the temple but also the king's palace lends credence to their use in official capacities. Also, although pottery sherds were present by the tens of thousands near and around the bakery, they were found only rarely in residential areas or other contexts further removed from the temple.

What is fascinating about the bakeries is how they reflect the Egyptian manner of industrial production. In our society, we would construct an industrial bakery based on the parameters of needed output: What and how much bread needs to be produced. Then, by scaling up the size of the mixers and ovens and implementing an assembly line, the product would be mass-produced, but not in Egypt. Although the first process, determining what and how much needed to be produced, was similar to our own, the means by which this was achieved was very different. The Egyptians knew that a standard oven could produce a certain number of loaves of bread. In their calculations, they simply multiplied the known, the standard domestic oven, as many times as needed to produce the quantities of bread desired. This system of production was common practice in Egypt. Labor was cheap, and thus, replication of existing production systems to meet larger needs only required the addition of a level of managers to reach the goal, organization rather than efficiency of labor being the standard solution to mass production. Through careful archaeology, not only was an inappropriately applied functional label corrected, but through the use of bakery scenes, a fuller understanding (and a degree of corroboration) was achieved, resulting in a better understanding of how Amarna worked as a royal city.

Barry Kemp's reconsideration of the function of a previously labeled area intersects a larger problem faced by all archaeologists working at sites with a long history of investigation: How best to compare data collected by different projects that employed different methodologies to investigate different goals. How we structure any comparison will impact our view of the past. For example, when frequency of animal bones, pottery sherds or lithics recovered from different stratigraphic levels or different parts of a site are compared, complications can arise through simple arithmetic computations. Figure 9.8 shows a graphic representation of domestic animal use from three different Amarna areas, based on data collected (at least in part) from early-twentieth-century excavations. The three graphs represent skeletal remains of three domestic food species recovered from two large homes and one area composed of smaller, presumably working class, homes. Because beef is considered an expensive or elite food throughout much of Egyptian history, it is

AMARNA ANIMAL USE

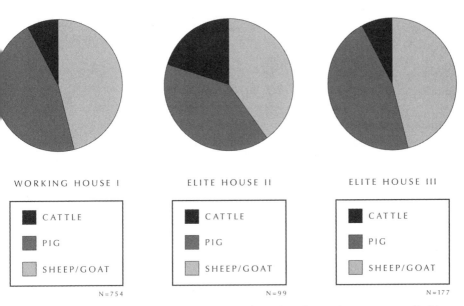

WORKING HOUSE I   ELITE HOUSE II   ELITE HOUSE III

CATTLE	CATTLE	CATTLE
PIG	PIG	PIG
SHEEP/GOAT	SHEEP/GOAT	SHEEP/GOAT

N=754   N=99   N=177

FIGURE 9.8. Graphic representation of animal use from three house sites at Amarna (Jackie Gardner after Payne 2011).

not surprising to see a larger proportion of cattle bones recovered from larger, presumably more wealthy, homes. But, is this graphic representation a true reflection of socially elite food preferences? Because actual numerical counts of the different animal bones are not reported, the validity of this common sense conclusion cannot be fully evaluated. It is curious to point out that one of the large homes produced a graphic display similar to that of the working class homes and the one large home where beef seems to be more dominant has a relatively small sample size (N = 99).

Herein lies an inherent problem in such comparisons. Figure 9.9 shows three house units with three species of animals represented. (The point of the example remains the same if we were discussing pottery sherds, lithics or any common artifact.) Percentage-based comparisons show that species 1 is less abundant between House 1 and House 2, then increases again in House 3. From this, one might surmise that activities associated with species 1 were less prevalent at House 2. However, if we look at Table 9.2, where the actual numerical values for the three species are presented, species 1 in fact increases across the site: from House 1 to House 2, and from House 2 to House 3. What has happened is that although species 1 increases, it does not do so at the same

HYPOTHETICAL ANIMAL USE

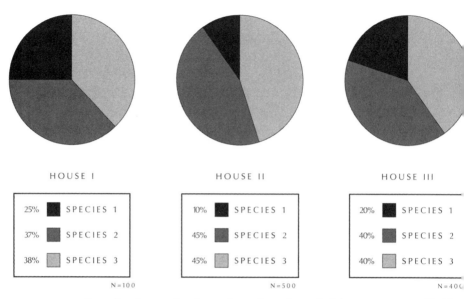

FIGURE 9.9. Example of reporting fauna from three theoretical house structures (Jackie Gardner).

rate as species 3, giving the impression when expressed as a percentage that it was decreasing in abundance.

Clearly, relative artifact abundances (percentages) may offer misleading evidence. These abundances may be correlated with the size of the samples from which they have been derived. Recall in our discussion on sampling (Chapter 2), as the size of the sample increases, the relative differences between artifact types change. Now, it may be that the changing abundances represent some real cultural phenomena, or it might be that changing abundances are an arithmetic product of the samples and their size. Note that in the real example from Amarna, the sample size for the house with a high percentage of cattle is relatively small compared to the other two. When the sample size

TABLE 9.2. *Numerical values for a hypothetical faunal assemblage recovered from three house structures*

	House 1	House 2	House 3
Species 1	25	50	80
Species 2	37	225	160
Species 3	38	225	160

increased, as in the second large house, the ratio of cattle to other animals is similar to that of smaller homes. The question that should be asked is: Do these graphs represent ancient food preferences, or is what we see a factor of sample size and the manner used to compare the samples?

There are simple statistical means by which to test for sample size effects, namely ranked order correlations where the actual counts of the artifacts are compared to their ranked order of abundance, but by simply making the actual counts of recovered artifacts available, common sense can often lead to the same cautionary questions posed here.

RECONSTRUCTING AKHETATEN

Returning again to Amarna, information gathered from archaeology and tomb scenes suggest that the ideal house was surrounded by a wall, which could reach as high as three meters. Within the compound were granaries, circular structures about 2.3 meters wide, with domed tops and a well. Sheds and enclosures of different kinds could be identified, as well as animal pens and gardens. In rich homes a shrine might be located within a formal garden. Rich houses also might have an apartment for a house manager or a family member. Kitchens, identified by small groups of circular clay ovens, were often positioned south or downwind of the house.

At Amarna, the houses of rich and poor can be separated by size more than by design, although smaller houses often lacked an entrance porch. If house size is an indication of social class, a profile of the community might be established. Kemp tabulated the data for Amarna and produced a frequency distribution (Figure 9.10) that mimics what one would expect from any community: an abundance of smaller homes, with a decreasing number of larger homes suggesting increasing wealth limited to fewer people.

Recreating a sense of how ancient Akhetaten functioned and actually may have looked involves interpreting archaeological, pictorial, and textual data in a mutually supportive role. Available evidence shows that most of the residential population lived in the Central City and the North Suburb. The king and family lived in a more-or-less secluded palace area north of the North Suburb and periodically commuted to the Central City to reside for the working day (or perhaps longer?) at the palace, to worship at the temple, and to deal with the day-to-day affairs of kingship. Many of the ministers and high officials also embarked on a commute to the central administrative area. The vizier, for example, lived some two kilometers to the south of the Central City, and other important officials, judging from house-size, lived even farther away. The point of interaction of the king and his officials seems, by all evidence, to be at the king's Central City house.

The king's house was at the center of a complex of buildings devoted to the business of governing the country. There was no wall to define the administrative palace, but a myriad of little offices extended around the king's house for those conducting business, thereby creating a palace of sorts. Little detail is available as to which departments might have occupied which offices or even areas. One exception is the "Bureau for the Correspondence of Pharaoh" within which was found the clay tablets known today as the Amarna Letters, archiving the diplomatic correspondence of the day. Based on bricks stamped "The House of Life" it appears a nearby structure was likely a repository for religious scrolls and other important documents that were kept for study or copying.

One important palace discovery was made on the ground level of an outside wall – a painted panel depicting bound captives. This same picture is shown in tomb paintings, where it is depicted positioned just below the "Window of Appearance." The Window must have been a balcony open to public view on one side and accessed on the other from the interior of the house. The purpose of the window seems to be for ceremonial gifting of gold and other precious objects to individuals held in high esteem and to announce the promotion of important officials. From one source (Horemheb Edict), it also appears that the window might have been used for regular distribution of rations. Anthropologically, the ceremonial distribution of rations to high officials would serve to reinforce their dependence on the king, and there is some tangential support for this proposition in that large storehouses and a granary were located in proximity to the Palace.

Tomb scenes also suggest a constant military presence around the king when he was in the public arena. Wherever the king goes, he seems to be accompanied by units from the army. This is supported by some parts of the Horemheb Edict, where a royal bodyguard is noted to be constantly changing. Interestingly, there is little archaeological evidence for any military architecture at Amarna. Near the North Palace, the supposed home of the king, were outlines of what might be barracks for the bodyguard, but there is nothing like this in the Central City or in the residential areas. From the tomb of Mahu, chief of the Medjay (police), we know that a chariot police was used to keep order within the city, but this was a separate and distinct force from the army. Near the edge of the Central City, there is a building that looks as if it might have included stables for horses and tethering stones, which is presumed to be the Medjay headquarters, but from the outside it appears

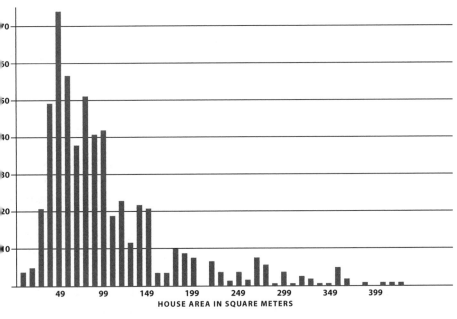

FIGURE 9.10. House-size distribution at Amarna (Ault and Flores after Kemp 1989, figure 101).

plain and unfortified. From this we might be able to deduce that although the army maintained a strong presence around the king, militarism was not a part of everyday life. Although a neighbor might be an officer in the army, he led a civilian lifestyle when off duty.

Although archaeology has given us the layout of the city, actual pictures of the city recorded in a number of rock-cut tombs provide an unusual look into ancient Egyptian aesthetics and the rhythm of life at Akhetaten. The mere fact that such a record exists offers important insights for reconstructing the town, even taking into consideration that the artist's perspective and purpose was far different than ours. The paintings show, for example, a number of building features that could not be determined archaeologically. They also show a city decorated with trees and gardens as well as splashes of color on buildings, which is a stark contrast to the nearly monochrome ruins we see today.

In summary, by combining information gleaned across a number of disciplines we can not only recreate life in Amarna with much more detail, but also shed additional light on questions typically beyond the reach of archaeological data alone. For example, from anthropology and the social sciences we have a better understanding of the role of monumental architecture in ancient Egyptian society. The emphasis on temples in the New Kingdom appears to be in concordance with social scientists' beliefs that monumental architecture is a means of projecting power and influence over the populace. The imposing buildings might indicate the need for the king and his surrogates to reconsolidate a hierarchical political order that was weakened during the Middle Kingdom and lost in the Second Intermediate Period. The temples served as a symbol of the power of the king and his deities, and through them touched the lives of every Egyptian.

Art history, philology, and architectural studies have added considerably to the depth of our understanding of the symbolic nature of temple structures and the temple's role in the life of the king and the populace. Art history has also added many details to our knowledge of how the city once looked and how it functioned. For example, judging from period tomb scenes, multi-level houses seem common among the elite, and because many houses have been shown archaeologically to have possessed an internal staircase, it seems likely that a roof access was a desirable feature.

We can now also say that unlike the Middle Kingdom, where there seemed to be some grid-style planning applied to streets and homes for all size of settlements, in the New Kingdom this seems to have been abandoned. Outside of the government sector houses were interlocked in complex patterns, with rich and poor living side by side, creating distinctive neighborhoods throughout the residential areas. Also, there seems to be no preferred house location other than frontage or access to one of the main thoroughfares, beyond which paths wound in and around buildings, homes, shops, granaries, and other structures. What is striking about the community and probably typical of the time are the refuse piles. Heaps of garbage were dumped everywhere, in alleys, on streets, near wells, and just about anywhere it could be dumped. Clearly, city living did not mimic the clean, orderly scenes recorded in tombs.

Summing up the city, its neighborhoods, and palace layout, one thing seems obvious: The vivid portrayal of Akhetaten, its king, and people could not have been possible without a complementary, cross-disciplinary approach.

10

ARCHAEOLOGY IN PERSPECTIVE

Having "traveled" through 100 millennia of Egyptian archaeology, the reader should by now realize that conducting archaeology in Egypt is a broad and diverse field of inquiry. Throughout the text, I have chosen to present the potential and limitations of some of the more common methods and techniques being employed today, rather than advocate a particular approach. Due to limits of space and time, many areas of archaeology are only touched on whereas others, such as underwater archaeology, remain totally unexplored. To fully do them justice would require another volume, yet the reader would find that even these specialized applications follow the same principles and goals of conventional archaeology.

One of the main goals of this book has been to explore the dual (and sometimes dueling) nature of archaeology as both history and science. Technological and theoretical advances notwithstanding, this essential dichotomy remains. Likewise, the actual practice of archaeological fieldwork has not changed *qualitatively* in the past century. Although some practitioners are concerned with how archaeology should be conducted and what it should seek to answer, the majority of field archaeologists working in Egypt have been and remain devoted not to large theoretical questions about why things changed, but to describing the past lifeways of the ancient Egyptians. Indeed, were Petrie to somehow be transported into the present-day, he would almost certainly be able to recognize and grasp current field archaeology. This is not to say, however, that such labors have been unfruitful; indeed, archaeologists have made great progress over the years in elucidating Egypt's past. We can see and describe how Egypt transformed from hunter-gatherers to village dwellers to the first great territorial state in history. Although we do not know the exact mechanisms behind these changes, we do know some of the key elements: population growth, environmental changes, technological innovations (particularly in food production), and competition from foreign cultures. Similarly, regardless of disciplinary debates and the championing of one paradigm over another, most archaeologists still employ evolutionary principles in their attempts to explain Egyptian cultural change. Although often unstated (but revealed by such terms as adaption and transformation), the theory of cultural evolution, first developed in the nineteenth century, is the underpinning for more complex explanations of cultural change involving social, environmental, and biological factors. Thus Egypt's rise from Paleolithic hunter-gatherers to egalitarian villagers to a complex nation-state ruled by a god-king is still most often explored as a relationship between environment and economics, with varying deference given to notions of free will, religion, and ideology in determining the eventual sociopolitical outcome.

Although a career in archaeology is probably not what many parents envision for their children when sending them off to college, it is a calling that can bring considerable satisfaction (but not necessarily money) to those fortunate enough to practice it. I am, as my mentor and close friend once said of himself, "one of those who remains convinced that to understand the great transformations our species has undergone through the millennia of existence is an indispensable part of a liberal arts education, and that a fundamental aspect of archaeology is that much of what we can hope to know about ourselves and our future can come from the study of the past. . . . Although the hard sciences can tell us much about the world we live in, archaeology has the potential to tell us where we came from and how we arrived at where we are today" (Wenke 1990).

I believe, however, that the discipline of archaeology as it is practiced in Egypt cannot stand alone. Rather, a comprehensive understanding of the multifaceted nature of the human experience can only be reached through cooperative research with our sister disciplines in geology, biology, paleontology, philology, and art history. Egypt's archaeological past – broken pieces of pottery, sand-blasted lithics, and architectural ruins – can come to life when art history's brightly painted murals and sculptures and philology's textual accounts of charismatic leaders, poets, brigands, and braggarts are set against the backdrop of a dynamic river and changing environment.

REFERENCES

Adams, B. (1995) *Ancient Nekhen: Garstang in the City of Hierakonpolis*. Egyptian Studies Association Publication 3. Surrey: SIA Publishing.

Adams, B. and K. Cialowicz (1997) *Protodynastic Egypt*. London: Shire Egyptology.

Adams, Robert McC. (1981) *Heartland of Cities: Surveys of Ancient Settlement and Land Use on the Central Floodplain of the Euphrates*. Chicago: University of Chicago Press.

Anati, E. (1999) "The Rock Art of the Negev Desert," *Near Eastern Archaeology*, 62(1): 22–34.

Arnold, D. and J. Bourriau (eds.) (1993) *An Introduction to Ancient Egyptian Pottery*, Deutsches Archäologisches Institut Abteilung Kairo Sondershrift 17. Mainz am Rhein: Philipp von Zabern.

Avni, G. (1991) "Survey of Deserted Bedouin Campsites in the Negev Highlands and Its Implications for Archaeological Research," in *Pastoralism in the Levant* (O. Bar-Yosef and A. Khazanov, eds.), pp. 241–254. Monographs in World Archaeology 10. Madison, WI: Prehistoric Press.

Baily, C. (1985) "Dating the Arrival of the Bedouin Tribes in the Sinai and the Negev," *Journal of the Economic and Social History of the Orient* 28(1): 20–49.

Bard, K. (ed.) (1999) *Encyclopedia of the Archaeology of Egypt*. London: Routledge.

Bates, O. (1914) *The Eastern Libyans: An Essay*. London: Macmillan.

Bell, B. (1970) "The Oldest Records of the Nile Floods," *The Geographical Journal* 136(4): 569–573.

———— (1971) "The Dark Ages in Ancient History I. The First Dark Age in Egypt," *American Journal of Archaeology* 75(1): 1–26.

———— (1975) "Climate and the History of Egypt: The Middle Kingdom," *American Journal of Archaeology*, 79(3): 223–269.

Bell, L. (1977) "The New Kingdom Divine Temple: The Example of Luxor," in *Temples of Ancient Egypt* (B. Shafer, ed.), pp. 127–184. Ithaca, NY: Cornell University Press.

Binford, L. R. (1964) "A Consideration of Archaeological Research Design," *American Antiquity* 4, pp. 425–441.

Bintliff, J. L. and C. F. Gaffney (1986) *Archaeology at the Interface: Studies in Archaeology's Relationships with History, Geography, Biology and Physical Science. British Archaeological Reports International Series 300.*

Bowman A. and E. Rogan (1999) "Agriculture in Egypt from Pharaonic to Modern Times," in *Agriculture in Egypt: From Pharaonic to Modern Times* (A. Bowman and E. Rogan, eds.), pp. 1–32. Oxford: Oxford University Press.

Breasted, J. H. (1988) *Ancient Records of Egypt Vols. I–V*. London: Histories and Mysteries of Man Ltd.

Brewer, D. J. (1987) "Seasonality in the Prehistoric Fayum Based on the Incremental Growth Structures of the Nile Catfish (Pisces: Clarias)," *Journal of Archaeological Science* 14, pp. 459–472.

——— (1989) *Fisherman, Hunters, and Herders: Zooarchaeology in the Fayum, Egypt.* British Archaeological Reports S478.

——— (1991) "Paleotemperatures in Predynastic Egypt Inferred from the Remains of the Nile Perch," *World Archaeology* 22(3): 288–303.

——— (2005) *Ancient Egypt: Foundations of a Civilization.* London: Pearson Education.

——— (2007) "Agriculture and Animal Husbandry," in *The Egyptian World* (T. Wilkinson, ed.), pp. 131–145, London: Routledge Press.

Brewer, D. J. and E. Teeter (2007) *Egypt and the Egyptians.* Cambridge: Cambridge University Press.

Brewer, D. J., D. Redford, and S. Redford (1994) *Domestic Plants and Animals: The Egyptian Origins.* Warminster, UK: Aris and Phillips.

Brewer, D. J., R. Wenke, J. Isaacson, D. Haag (1996) "Mendes Regional Archaeology Survey and Remote Sensing Analysis," *Sahara* 8: 29–42.

Brown, A. G. (1997) *Alluvial Geoarchaeology: Floodplain Archaeology and Environmental Change* (Cambridge Manuals in Archaeology). New York: Cambridge University Press.

Brunton, Guy (1928) *The Badarian Civilisation.* London: Quaritch.

Burnbury, Judith and Angus Graham (nd) *Nekhen: Island origins and the migrating Nile.* (Manuscript, 1 page.)

Butzer, K. (1959a) "Some Recent Geological Deposits of the Egyptian Nile Valley," *The Geographical Journal* 125: 75–79.

——— (1959b) *Die Naturlandschaft Aegyptens waehrend der Vorgeschichte und dem Dynastischen Zeitalter.* Akademie der Wissenschaften und der Literatur (Mainz), Abhandl. Math.-Nat. Kl. 1959, No. 2. 80 pp. Wiesbaden.

——— (1976) *Early Hydraulic Civilizations: A Study in Cultural Ecology.* Chicago: University of Chicago Press.

Cagle, A. (2003) *The Spatial Structure of Kim el-Hisn: An Old Kingdom Town in the Western Nile Delta, Egypt.* British Archaeological Reports International Series 1099. Oxford, Archaeopress.

Caton-Thompson, G. and E. W. Gardner (1934) *The Desert Fayum.* London: The Royal Anthropological Institute of Great Britain and Ireland.

Champion, T. C. (2003) "Egypt and the Diffusion of Culture," in *Views of Egypt since Napoleon Bonaparte: Imperialism, Colonialism and Modern Appropriations* (D. Jeffreys, ed.), pp. 127–145. London: UCL Press.

Childe, V. G. (1936) *Man Makes Himself.* Oxford: Oxford University Press.

——— (1956) *New Light on the Most Ancient East.* 4th ed. London: Routledge and Kegan Paul.

Chmielewski, W. (1968) "Early and Middle Paleolithic Sites near Arkin, Sudan," in *Prehistory of Nubia* (F. Wendorf, ed.), pp. 110–193. Dallas: Fort Burguin Research Center.

Close, A. (ed.) (1986) *The Wadi Kubbaniya Skeleton: A Late Paleolithic Burial in Southern Egypt.* Dallas: SMU Press.

Copi, I. M. (1968) *Introduction to Logic,* 3rd edition. London: Macmillan.

Crocker, P. (1985) "Status Symbols in the Architecture of El-'Amarna," *Journal of Egyptian Archaeology* 71: 52–65.

Darwin, Charles (1859) *The Origin of Species.* New York: Random House Edition, 1979.

Davies, N. de G. (1905) *The Rock Tombs of el Amarna II.* London: Egypt Exploration Fund.

——— (1908) *The Rock Tombs of el Amarna V.* London: Egypt Exploration Fund.

Davis, V. and R. Friedman (1998) *Egypt Uncovered.* London: British Museum Press.

Debono, F. and B. Mortensen (1990) *El Omari: A Neolithic Settlement and Other Sites in the Vicinity of Wadi Hof Helwan.* Mainz am Rhein: Philipp von Zabern.

Devers, W. (1992) "Pastoralism and the End of the Urban Early Bronze Age in Palestine," in *Pastoralism in the Levant* (O. Bar-Yosef and A. Khazanov, eds.), pp. 83–92. Madison, WI: Prehistory Press.

Dreyer, G. (1992a) "Recent Discoveries in the U-Cemetery at Abydos," in *The Nile Delta in Transition: 4th–3rd Millennium BC* (E. van den Brink, ed.), pp. 293–300. Jerusalem: Israeli Exploration Society.

———— (1992b) "Horus Krokodil, ein Gegenkönig der Dynastie 0," in *The Followers of Horus, Studies in Honor of Michael Allen Hoffman* (R. Friedman and B. Adams, eds.), pp. 259–263. Oxford: Oxbow Press.

Dreyer, G., V. Hartung, T. Hikade, C. Köhler, V. Müller and F. Pumpenmeier (1998) "Umm el-Qaab, Nachuntersuchungen im frühzeitlichen Königsfriedhof 9/1/ Vorbericht," *Mitteilungen des Deutschen Archäologischen Instituts, Abteilung Kairo*, Wiesbaden 54:79–165.

Dunnell, R. (1971) *Systematics in Prehistory.* New York: Free Press.

———— (1978) "Style and Function: A Fundamental Dichotomy," *American Antiquity* 43(2): 192–202.

Eiwanger, J. (1984) "Merimde-Benisaläme I: Die Funde der Urschicht," *Archäologische Veröffentlichungen* 47. Mainz am Rhein: Philipp von Zabern.

———— (1988) "Merimde-Benisaläme II: Die Funde der Mittleren," *Archäologische Veröffentlichungen* 51. Mainz am Rhein: Philipp von Zabern.

———— (1992) "Merimde-Benisaläme III: Die Funde der Jüngeren," *Archäologische Veröffentlichungen* 47. Mainz am Rhein: Philipp von Zabern.

Encyclopedia Britannica (eb.com) Entry: Giuseppe Fiorelli. Accessed November 11, 2010.

Faltings, D. (1998) "Ergebnisse der neuen Ausgrabungen in Buto, Chronologie und Fernbeziehungen der Buto-Maadi-Kultur neu überdacht," in *Stationen: Beiträge zur Kulturgeschichte Ägyptens (Festschrift R. Stadelmann)* (H. Guksch and D. Polz, eds.), S. 35–45. Mainz, P. von Zabern.

Feinman, G., S. Kwaleski, and R. Blanton (1984) "Modelling Ceramic Production and Organizational Change in the Pre-Hispanic Valley of Oaxaca, Mexico," in *The Many Dimensions of Pottery: Ceramics in Archaeology and Anthropology* (S. E. van der Leeuw and A. C. Pritchard, eds.), pp. 295–333. Amsterdam: Universiteit van Amsterdam.

Finkelstein, I. and A. Perevolotsky (1990) "Processes of Sedentarization and Nomadization in the History of Sinai and the Negev," *Bulletin of the American Schools of Oriental Research* 279: 67–88.

Franke, D. (2001) "Middle Kingdom," in *The Oxford Encyclopedia of Ancient Egypt* (D. Redford, ed.), pp. 393–400. Oxford: Oxford University Press.

Frankfort, H. (1927) "Preliminary Report on the Excavations at Tell el-Amarna, 1926–7," *The Journal of Egyptian Archaeology* 13: 209–218.

Friedman, R. (1994) *Predynastic settlement ceramics of Upper Egypt: A comparative study of the ceramics of Hemamieh, Nagada, and Hierakonpolis.* PhD Dissertation. Ann Arbor, Michigan: University Microfilms.

———— (1996) "The Ceremonial Centre at Hierakonpolis Locality HK29A," in *Aspects of Early Egypt* (J. Spencer, ed.), pp. 16–35. London: British Museum.

Fritz, J. and F. Plog (1970) "The Nature of Archaeological Explanation," *American Antiquity* 35(4): 405–412.

Gardiner, A. (1937) *Late Egyptian Miscellanies* 7, Bibliotheca Aegyptiaca. Brussels: Edition de la Foundation Egyptologique Reine Elisabeth.

Geller, J. (1992) *Predynastic beer production at Hierakonpolis, Upper Egypt: Archaeological evidence and anthropological implications*. PhD Dissertation. Ann Arbor, Michigan: University Microfilms.

Ginter, B. and J. Kozlowski (1979) "Excavation Report on the Prehistoric and Predynastic Settlement in el-Tarif during 1978," Mitteilungen des Deutschen Archäologischen Instituts, Abteilung Kairo, Wiesbaden 35, pp. 87–102.

———— (1984) "The Tarifian and the Origin of the Naqadian," in *Origin and Early Development of Food-Producing Cultures in North-Eastern Africa* (L. Krzyzaniak and M. Kobusiewicz, eds.), pp. 247–260. Poznan, Poland: Poznan Archaeological Museum.

Ginter, B., J. Kozlowski, and B. Drobniewicz (1979) *Silexindustrien von El Tarif*. Mainz am Rhein: Philipp von Zabern.

Godley, A. D. (trans.) (1990) *Herodotus*. Cambridge: Loeb.

Goodman, S., J. Hobbs, and D. Brewer (1992) "Nimr Cave: Holocene Animal Remains from a Site in the Egyptian Eastern Desert," *Paleoecology of Africa* 23, pp. 73–90.

Grajetzki, W. (2006) *The Middle Kingdom of Ancient Egypt*. London: Duckworth.

Haiman, M. (1996) "Early Bronze Age IV Settlement Pattern of the Negev and Sinai Deserts: View from Small Marginal Temporary Sites," *Bulletin of the American Schools of Oriental Research* 303, pp. 1–32.

Hassan, F. (1979) "Geoarchaeology: The Geologist and Archaeology," *American Antiquity* 44, pp. 267–279.

———— (1986a) "Holocene Lakes and Prehistoric Settlements of the Western Faiyum, Egypt," *Journal of Archaeological Science* 13, pp. 483–501.

———— (1986b) "Desert Environment and the Origins of Agriculture in Egypt," *Norwegian Archaeological Review* 19, pp. 63–76.

———— (1997a) "The Dynamics of a Riverine Civilization: A Geoarchaeological Perspective on the Nile Valley," *World Archaeology* 29, pp. 51–74.

———— (1997b) "Nile Floods and Political Disorder in Early Egypt," in *Third Millennium BC Climate Change and Old World Collapse* (H. Nüzhet Dalfes, G. Kukla, and H. Weiss, eds.), pp. 1–24. New York: Springer.

———— (1999) "Nagada," in *Encyclopedia of the Archaeology of Egypt* (K. Bard, ed.), pp. 555–557. London: Routledge.

———— (2010) "A River Runs through Egypt: Nile Floods and Civilization," *Geotimes* 50(4): 22–25.

Hassan, F. and B. Stucki (1987) "Nile Floods and Climatic Change," in *Climate: History, Periodicity, and Predictability*," (M. R. Rampino, J. Sanders, W. Newman, and L. K. Königsson, eds.), pp. 37–46. New York: Van Nostrand Reinhold.

Hassanein Bey, A. M. (1924) "Crossing the Untraversed Libyan Desert," *National Geographic Magazine* 46(3): 235–277.

Hegmon, M. (1992) "Archaeological Research on Style," *Annual Review of Anthropology* 21, pp. 517–536.

Henrickson, E. and M. McDonald (1983) "Ceramic Form and Function: An Ethnographic Search and an Archeological Application," *American Anthropologist, New Series* 85, pp. 630–645.

Hodder, I. (1985) "Post Processual Archaeology," in *Advances in Archaeological Method and Theory* 8 (M. Schiffer, ed.), pp. 1–26. New York: Academic Press.

Hoffman, M. A. (1982) *The Predynastic of Hierakonpolis: An Interim Report. Egyptian Studies Association Publication 1*. Egypt: Cairo University Herbarium, and Macomb: Western Illinois University.

———— (1984) *Egypt before the Pharaohs*. London: Ark.

Hole, F. (1979) "Prediscovering the Past in the Present: Ethnoarchaeology in Luristan, Iran," in *Ethnoarchaeology* (Carol Kramer, ed.), pp. 176–191. New York: Columbia University Press.

Holmes, D. L. (1989) *The Predynastic Lithic Industries of Upper Egypt: A Comparative Study of the Lithic Traditions of Badari, Nagada, and Hierakonpolis (Vols. I–II., British Archaeological Reports, International Series.)* Cambridge Monographs in Archaeology, 33.

―――― (1993) "Rise of the Nile Delta," *Nature* 363, pp. 402–403.

Holmes, D. and R. Friedman (1994) "Survey and Test Excavations in the Badari Region," *Proceedings of the Prehistoric Society* 60, pp. 105–142.

Hopkins, D. (1993) "Pastoralists in Late Bronze Age Palestine: Which Way Did They Go?" *The Biblical Archaeologist,* 56(4): 200–211.

Huffman, T. (2004) "Beyond Data: The Aim and Practice of Archaeology," *The South African Archaeological Bulletin* 59(180): 66–69.

Hurst, H. (1952) *The Nile.* London: Constable.

Jeffreys, D. (2003) "Introduction: Two Hundred Years of Ancient Egypt: Modern History and Ancient Archaeology," in *Views of Egypt since Napoleon Bonaparte: Imperialism, Colonialism and Modern Appropriations* (D. Jeffreys, ed.), pp.1–18. London: UCL Press.

Joukowsky, M. (1980) *A Complete Manual of Field Archaeology.* Englewood Cliffs, New Jersey: Prentice Hall, Inc.

Kaiser, W. (1957) "Zur Inneren Chronologie der Naqadakultur," *Archaeologia Geographica* 6, pp. 69–77.

Kaiser, W. and G. Dreyer 1982. "Umm el Qaab: Nachuntersuchungen im frühzeitlichen Königsfriedhof'. *Mitteilungen des Deutschen Archäologische Instituts, Abteilung Kairo, Wiesbaden* 38: 211–269.

Kees, H. (1961) *Ancient Egypt: A Cultural Topography* (F. D. Ian, trans.). Chicago: University of Chicago Press.

Keita, S. (2003) "A Study of Vault Porosities in Early Upper Egypt from the Badarian through Dynasty 1," *World Archaeology* 35, pp. 210–222.

Kemp, B. (1976) "The Window of Appearance at El-Amarna, and the Basic Structure of the City," *The Journal of Egyptian Archaeology* 62, pp. 81–99.

―――― (1977a) "The Early Development of Towns in Egypt," *Antiquity* 51, pp. 185–200.

―――― (1977b) "The City of El-Amarna as a Source for the Study of Urban Society in Ancient Egypt," *World Archaeology* 9(2): 123–139.

―――― (1983) "Old Kingdom, Middle Kingdom and Second Intermediate Period," in *Ancient Egypt: A Social History* (B. G Trigger, B. J. Kemp, D. O'Connor, and A. B. Lloyd, eds.), pp. 71–182. Cambridge: Cambridge University Press.

―――― (1987) "The Amarna Workmen's Village in Retrospect," *The Journal of Egyptian Archaeology* 73, pp. 21–50.

―――― (1989) *Ancient Egypt: Anatomy of a Civilization.* London: Routledge.

Kemp, B. J. and S. Garfi (1993) *A Survey of the Ancient City of El-Amarna.* Occasional Publications 9, London: Egypt Exploration Society.

Khun, T. (1962) *The Structure of Scientific Revolutions.* Chicago: University of Chicago Press.

Kitchen, K. (1990) "The Arrival of the Libyans in the Late New Kingdom Egypt," in *Libya and Egypt* (A. Leahy, ed.), pp. 15–27. London: Society of Libyan Studies.

Kozlowski, J. and B. Ginter (1989) "The Fayum Neolithic in the Light of New Discoveries," in *Late Prehistory of the Nile Basin and Sahara* (L. Krzyzaniak and M. Kobusiewicz, eds.), pp. 157–179. Poznan, Poland: Poznan Archaeological Museum.

Kramer, C. (1979) "Introduction," in *Ethnoarchaeology* (C. Kramer, ed.), pp. 1–20. New York: Columbia University Press.

Kreiger, A. D. (1944) "The Typological Concept," *American Antiquity* 9, pp. 271–288.

Kroeber, A. L. (1916) "Zuni Potsherds," *Anthropological Papers of the American Museum of Natural History* 18(1): 1–17. New York: American Museum of Natural History.

Kroeper, K. (1992) "Tombs of Elite in Minshat Abu Omar," in *The Nile Delta in Transition: 4th–3rd Millennium BC* (E. van den Brink, ed.), pp.127–150. Jerusalem: Israeli Exploration Society.

Kroeper, K. and D. Wildung (1985) *Minshat Abu Omar*, Münchner Ost-Delta Expedition, Vorbericht 1978–1984. Munich: Staatliche Ägyptischer Kunst.

Leek, F. (1972) "Teeth and Bread in Ancient Egypt," *Journal of Egyptian Archaeology* 58, pp. 126–132.

—— (1983) "Tooth Wear as Observed in Ancient Egyptian Skulls," *Journal of Human Evolution* 12, pp. 617–629.

Lehner, M. (1997) *The Complete Pyramids*. London: Thames and Hudson.

—— (2002) "The Pyramid Age Settlement of the Southern Mount at Giza," *Journal of the American Research Center in Egypt* 39: pp. 27–74.

Levy, T., E. R. B. Adams, and A. Muniz (2004) "Archaeology and the Shasu Nomads: Recent Excavations in the Jabal Hamrat Fidan, Jordan," in *Le-David Maskill: A Birthday Tribute for David Noel Freedman* (W. Propp and R. E. Friedman, eds.), pp. 63–89. Biblical and Judaic Studies from the University of California San Diego, 9. Winona Lake, Indiana: Eisenbrauns.

Lyell, C. (1830–1933) *Principles of Geology, Vols. I–III.* Chicago: University of Chicago Press Edition, 1999.

Marks, A. (1968a) "The Mousterian Industries of Nubia," in *The Prehistory of Nubia* I (F. Wendorf, ed.), pp. 194–314. Dallas: Fort Burguin Research Center.

—— (1968b) "The Khormusan: An Upper Pleistocene Industry in Sudanese Nubia," in *The Prehistory of Nubia* I (F. Wendorf, ed.), pp. 319–391. Dallas: Fort Burguin Research Center.

—— (1968c) "The Halfan Industry," in *The Prehistory of Nubia* I (F. Wendorf, ed.), pp. 392–460. Dallas: Fort Burguin Research Center.

—— (1968d) "The Sebilian Industry of the Second Cataract," in *The Prehistory of Nubia* I (F. Wendorf, ed.), pp. 461–531. Dallas: Fort Burguin Research Center.

Masali, M. (1972) "Body Size and Proportions as Revealed by Bone Measurements and Their Meaning in Environmental Adaptation," *Journal of Human Evolution* 1, pp. 187–197.

Masali, M. and B. Chiarelli (1972) "Demographic Data on the Remains of Ancient Egyptians," *Journal of Human Evolution* 1, pp. 161–169.

McHugh, W. P. (1974) "Late Prehistoric Cultural Adaptation in Southwest Egypt and the Problem of the Nilotic Origins of Saharan Cattle Pastoralism," *Journal of the American Research Center in Egypt* XI, pp. 2–29.

—— (1975) "Some Archaeological Results of the Bagnold-Mond Expedition to the Gilf Kebir and Gebel Uweinat, Southern Libyan Desert," *Journal of Near Eastern Studies* 34, pp. 31–62.

Meskell, Lynn (2002) *Private Life in New Kingdom Egypt*. Princeton, NJ: Princeton University Press.

Midant-Reynes, B. (2000) *The Prehistory of Egypt: From the First Egyptians to the First Pharaohs.* (I. Shaw, trans.). Oxford: Blackwell.

Morgan, C. (1973) "Archaeology and Explanation," *World Archaeology* 4(3): 259–276.

Murray, G. W. (1951) "The Egyptian Climate: An Historical Outline," *The Geographical Journal* 117, pp. 422–434.

Murnane, W. J. and C.C. van Siclen III (1993) *The Boundary Stelae of Akhenaten*. London: Kegan Paul.

Murray, T. (2002) "Evaluating Evolutionary Archaeology," *World Archaeology* 34(1): 47–59.

O'Connor, D. (1990) "The Nature of Tjemhu (Libyan) Society in Later New Kingdom Egypt," in *Libya and Egypt c. 1300–750 BC* (A. Leahy, ed.), pp. 29–114. London: Society for Libyan Studies.

Orton, C. (2000) *Sampling in Archaeology*. Cambridge: Cambridge University Press.

Payne, S. (2011) Zooarchaeology at Amarna, 2004–2005. Amarna Project (www.amarnaproject.com/pages/recent_projects/faunal_human/zooarchaeology.shtml).

Pendelbury, J. D. S. (1933) "Preliminary Report of the Excavations at Tell el Amarna 1932–1933," *Journal of Egyptian Archaeology* 19, pp. 113–118.

——— (1934) "Excavations at Tell el Amarna: Preliminary Report for the Season 1933–4," *Journal of Egyptian Archaeology* 20, pp. 129–136.

——— (1935) *Tell el-Amarna*. London: Lovat Dickson and Thompson Ltd.

——— (1951) *The City of Akhenaten* (Part III). London: Egypt Exploration Society.

Petrie, W. M. F. (1901) *Diospolis Parva*. London: Egyptian Exploration Fund 37.

——— (1904) *Methods and Aims in Archaeology*. London: Macmillan and Co.

——— (1921) *Corpus of Prehistoric Pottery and Palettes*. London: Bernard Quaritch.

——— (1931) *Seventy Years in Archaeology*. London: S. Low, Marston & Co.

——— (1953) *Ceremonial Slate Palettes: Corpus of Protodynastic Egypt*. London: British School of Archaeology.

Petrie, W. M. F. and J. E. Quibell (1896) *Naqada and Ballas*. London: Bernard Quaritch.

Puech, P., C. Serratrice, and F. Leek (1983) "Tooth Wear as Observed in Ancient Egyptian Skulls," *Journal of Human Evolution* 12, pp. 617–629.

Quibell, J. E. (1898) "Slate Palettes from Hierakonpolis," *Zeitschrift der für ägyptische Sprache und Altertumskunde*, S36: 81–84. Berlin.

——— (1900) *Hierakonpolis I*. London: Bernard Quaritch.

——— (1904–5) *Archaic Objects I–II*. Cairo: l'Institut français d'archéologie orientale.

Quibell, J. E. and F. W. Green (1902) *Hierakonpolis II*. London: Bernard Quaritch.

Raikes, R. L. and A. Palmiere (1972) "Environmental Conditions in the Nile Valley over the Past 10,000 Years," *Journal of Human Evolution* 1, pp. 147–154.

Ranke, H. (1925) *Alter und Herkunft der Löwenjagd Palette*. Heidelberg: Winter.

Raue, D. C. von Pilgrim, M. Bommas, R. Cortopassi, A. von den Driesch, D. Keller, T. Hikade, P. Kopp, J. Peters, B. von Pilgrim, S. Schaten, T. Schmidtz, M. Schultz, S. J. Seidlmayer (2004) Report on the 33rd Season of Excavation and Restoration on the Island of Elephantine. www.dainst.org/sites/default/files/medien/daik_ele33_rep_en.pdf?ft=all.

Redford, D. B. (1973) "Studies in Relations between Palestine and Egypt during the First Millennium BC: II. The Twenty-Second Dynasty," *Journal of the American Oriental Society* 93(1): 3–17.

——— (1992) *Egypt, Canaan and Israel*. Princeton, NJ: Princeton University Press.

Redford, S. and D. Redford (1989) "Graffiti and Petroglyphs Old and New from the Eastern Desert," *Journal of the American Research Center in Egypt* 26, pp. 3–50.

Rice, P. M. (1987) *Pottery Analysis: A Source Book*. Chicago: University of Chicago Press.

Riehl, S., R. Byrson, and P. Konstantin (2008) "Changing Growing Conditions for Crops during the Near Eastern Bronze Age (3000–1200 BC): The Stable Carbon Isotope Evidence," *Journal of Archaeological Science* 35, pp. 1011–1022.

Rizkana, I. and J. Seeher (1987) *Maadi: The Pottery of the Predynastic Settlement*. Mainz am Rhein: Philipp von Zabern.

Rosen, A. M. (1986) "Environmental Change and Settlement at Tel Lachish, Israel," *Bulletin of the American Schools of Oriental Research* 263, pp. 55–63.

Rosen, S. A. (1988) "Notes on the Origins of Pastoral Nomadism: A Case Study from the Negev and Sinai," *Current Anthropology* 29(3): 498–506.

_____ (1992a) "Nomads in Archaeology: A Response to Finkelstein and Perevolotsky," *Bulletin of the American Schools of Oriental Research* 287, pp. 75–85.

_____ (1992b) "The Case for Seasonal Movement of Pastoral Nomads in the Late Byzantine/ Early Arabic Period in the South Central Negev," in *Pastoralism in the Levant* (O. Bar-Yosef and A. Khazanov, eds.), pp. 153–164. Monographs in World Archaeology 10, pp. 241–254. Madison, WI: Prehistoric Press.

Rosen, S. and A. Gideon (1993) "The Edge of the Empire: The Archaeology of Pastoral Nomads in the Southern Negev Highlands in Late Antiquity," *The Biblical Archaeologist* 56(4): 189–199.

Rothenberg, B. (1979) *Sinai.* New York: Joseph J. Binns.

Saad, Z. (1951) *Royal Excavations at Helwan (1945–1947).* Supplément aux Annales du Service des Antiquités de l'Egypte Cahier 14. Cairo: Imprimerie de l'Institut français d'archeologie orientale.

Seeher, J. (1990) "Maadi eine prädynastische Kulturgruppe zwischen Oberägypten und Palästina," *Prähistorische Zeitschrift* 65(2): 123–56.

_____ (1999) "Maadi and Wadi Digla," in *Encyclopedia of the Archaeology of Egypt* (K. Bard, ed.), pp. 455–458. London: Routledge.

Seidlmayer, S. J. (1996) "Town and State in the Early Old Kingdom: A View from Elephantine," in *Aspects of Early Egypt* (J. Spencer, ed.), pp. 108–127. London: British Museum Press.

Shanks, M. and C. Tilley (1992) *Reconstructing Archaeology Theory and Practice.* London: Routledge.

Smith, W. (1949) *A History of Egyptian Sculpture and Painting in the Old Kingdom*, 2nd ed., London: Oxford University Press.

Smyntyna, O. V. (2003) "The Environmental Approach to Prehistoric Studies: Concepts and Theories," *History and Theory* 42, pp. 44–59.

Snape, S. (1996) *Egyptian Temples.* Buckinghamshire, Shire Publications Ltd.

_____ (2003) "The Emergence of Libya on the Horizon of Egypt," in *Mysterious Lands* (D. O'Connor and S. Quirke, eds.), pp. 93–106. London: University College London Press.

Spencer, A. J. 1993. *Early Egypt.* London: British Museum.

Spier, L. (1917) "An Outline for a Chronology of Zuni Ruins," *Anthropological Papers of the American Museum of Natural History* 18. New York: American Museum of Natural History.

Stanley, D. J. and A. G. Warne (1993a) "Nile Delta: Recent Geological Evolution and Human Impact," *Science* 260, pp. 628–634.

_____ (1993b) "Sea Level and Initiation of Predynastic Culture in the Nile Delta," *Nature* 363, pp. 435–438.

Steibing, W. (1971) "Hyksos Burials in Palestine: A Review of the Evidence," *Journal of Near Eastern Studies*, 30(2): 110–117.

Taylor, W. W. (1948) *A Study of Archaeology.* Carbondale: Southern Illinois University.

Teeter, E. (ed.) (2010) *Before the Pyramids: The Origins of the Egyptian Civilization.* Chicago: Oriental Institute.

Testart, A. (1982) *Les chasseurs-cueilleurs ou l' origine des inégalités.* Paris: Société d'Ethnographie.

Thomas, A. (1984) "Morphology and Affinities of the Nazlet Khater Man," *Journal of Human Evolution* 13, pp. 287–296.

Tixier, J. (1963) "Typologie de l'Epipaléolithique du Maghreb," *Mémoires du Centre de Recherches Anthropologiques, Préhistoriques et Ethnographiques, Alger.* 2. Paris, France.

Trigger, B. (1983) *Ancient Egypt: A Social History.* Cambridge: Cambridge University Press.

_____ (1990) "Monumental Architecture: A Thermodynamic Explanation of Symbolic Behavior," *World Archaeology* 22(2): 119–132.

_____ (1993) *Early Civilizations: Ancient Egypt in Context.* Cairo: American University in Cairo Press.

van den Brink, E. C. M. (1988) "The Amsterdam University Survey Expedition to the Northeastern Nile Delta (1984–1986); with a Contribution by Willem van Zeist," in *The Archaeology of the Nile Delta, Egypt: Problems and Priorities* (E. van den Brink, ed.), pp. 65–114. Amsterdam: Netherlands Foundation for Archaeological Research in Egypt.

van den Brink, E. C. M. (ed.) (1988) *The Archaeology of the Nile Delta, Egypt: Problems and Priorities.* Cairo: Netherland Institute of Archaeology.

_____ (ed.) (1992) *The Delta in Transition: 4th–3rd Millennium BC.* Jerusalem: Israeli Exploration Society.

Vermeersch, P. (1978) *L'Elkabien, Epipaléolithique de la Vallée du Nil Egyptien.* Fondation Égyptologique Reine Élisabeth, Universitaire Pers Leuven.

Vermeersch, P., G. Gijselings, and E. Paulissen (1984) "Discovery of the Nazlet Khater Man, Upper Egypt," *Journal of Human Evolution* 13, pp. 281–286.

Vermeersch, P., E. Paulissen, S. Stokes, S. Charhier, C. Van Peer, C. Stinger, and W. Lindsay (1998) "A Middle Palaeolithic Burial of a Modern Human at Taramsa Hill, Egypt," *Antiquity* 72, pp. 475–484.

von der Way, T. (1986) "Tel el Fara'in Buto 1," Bericht. *Mitteilungen des Deutschen Archäologischen Instituts, Abteilung Kairo* Mitteilungen des Deutschen Archäologischen Instituts, Abteilung Kairo, Wiesbaden 42, pp. 191–212.

_____ (1987) "Tel el Fara'in-Buto 2," Bericht mit einem Beitrag von Klaus Schmidt zu den lithischen Kleinfunden. *Mitteilungen des Deutschen Archäologischen Instituts, Abteilung Kairo* Mitteilungen des Deutschen Archäologischen Instituts, Abteilung Kairo, Wiesbaden 43, pp. 241–250.

_____ (1992) "Excavations at Tell el-Fara'in/Buto 1987–1989," in *The Delta in Transition: 4th–3rd Millennium BC* (E. C. M. van den Brink, ed.), pp. 1–10. Jerusalem: Israeli Exploration Society.

_____ (1993) "Untersuchungen zur Spätvor-und Frühgeschichte Unterägyptens," *SAGA* 8. Heidelberg.

Waddell, W. G. (trans.) (1948) *Manetho.* Loeb Classic Library. Cambridge, MA: Harvard University Press.

Wainwright, G. A. (1962) "The Meshwesh," *The Journal of Egyptian Archaeology* 48, pp. 89–99.

Ward, W. (1972) "The Shasu 'Bedouin': Notes on a Recent Publication," *Journal of the Economic and Social History of the Orient* 15, pp. 35–60.

Wendorf, F. W. (1968) *The Prehistory of Nubia Vols. I–II.* Dallas: Fort Burguin Research Center.

Wendorf, F. W. and R. Schild (1975) "The Paleolithic of the Lower Nile Valley," in *Problems in Prehistory: North Africa and the Levant* (F. W. Wendorf and A. E. Marks, eds.), pp. 127–169. Dallas: SMU Press.

_____ (1976) *Prehistory of the Nile Valley.* New York: Academic Press.

_____ (1980) *Prehistory of Eastern Sahara.* New York: Academic Press.

Wendorf, F. W., R. Schild, and A. Close (1980) *Loaves and Fishes: The Prehistory of Wadi Kubbanyia.* Dallas: SMU Press.

Wendorf, F. W., R. Schild, and A. Close (eds.) (1984) *Cattle Keepers of the Eastern Sahara: The Neolithic of Bir Kiseiba.* Dallas: SMU Press.

_____ (1989) *The Prehistory of Wadi Kubbanyia III: Late Paleolithic Archaeology.* Dallas: SMU Press.

Wengrow, D. (2006) *The Archaeology of Early Egypt: Social Transformations in North-East Africa 10000 to 2650 BC.* Cambridge: Cambridge University Press.

Wenke, R. J. (1989) "Egypt: Origins of Complex Societies," *Annual Review of Anthropology* 18, pp. 129–155.

_____ (1990) *Patterns in Prehistory.* Oxford: Oxford University Press.

———— (1997) "City-States, Nation States, and Territorial States: The Problem of Egypt," in *The Archaeology of City States: Cross-Cultural Approaches* (D. L. Nichols and T. H. Charlton, eds.), pp. 27–49. Washington and London: Smithsonian Institution Press.

———— (2009) *The Ancient Egyptian State*. Cambridge: Cambridge University Press.

Wenke, R. J., P. Buck, H. Hamroush, M. Kobusiewicz, K. Kroeper, and R. Redding (1988) "Kom el-Hisn: Excavation of an Old Kingdom Settlement in the Egyptian Delta," *Journal of the American Research Center in Egypt* 25, pp. 5–34.

Wenke, R. J., J. Long, and P. E. Buck (1988) "Epipaleolithic and Neolithic Subsistence and Settlement in the Fayyum Oasis of Egypt," *Journal of Field Archaeology* 15, pp. 29–51.

Wente, E. (1963) "Shekelesh or Shasu," *Journal of Near Eastern Studies* 22(3): 167–172.

Wilkinson, T. (2003) *Genesis of the Pharaohs: Dramatic New Discoveries Rewrite the Origins of Ancient Egypt*. London: Thames & Hudson.

Willey, G. and P. Phillips (1958) *Method and Theory in American Archaeology*. Chicago: University of Chicago Press.

Wilson, J. (1960) "A Civilization without Cities," in *City Invincible* (C. Kraeling and R. Adams, eds.). Chicago: University of Chicago Press.

Winkler, H. (1938–1939). *The Rock Drawings of Southern Egypt I-II*. London: Egypt Exploration Society.

Worschech, U. (1977) "Egypt and Moab," *Biblical Archaeologist* 60(4): 229–236.

Ziermann, M. (1993) Elephantine 16. Befestigungsanlagen und Stadtentwicklung in der Frühzeit und im frühen Alten Reich. AV 87. Mainz am Rhein, P. von Zabern.

INDEX